SYLVIA BURCH

"I WANT CHOCOLATE CAKE FOR DINNER!":
LET NURSING ROCK YOUR WORLD!

Contents

Cover

Title

Copyright

Dedication

Introduction

1. Nursing Can Be a Wild Ride!
2. How It All Started
3. Bringing It On — Slowly
4. Office Work 101
5. Making a Difference
6. Go Army!
7. A Recovering Nurse
8. And Beyond...

About the Author

Back Cover

Dedication

"Honey, you're going to have to publish that book!"

To Bill and his wonderful wife, Dot - and all the wonderful patients and caregivers who have inspired me and believed in my ability to help them. In reality, they have helped me beyond measure. There is no work on earth that is better than the art of nursing!

When I made my case management visits to Bill's home, I always ended my visit by completing the endless documentation and putting the different pages of his nursing care notes in a big binder that got fatter week by week. Bill would say to me, "Honey, you're going to have to publish that book!!"

The inspiration he gave me, however, was to put into words just how special the work of a nurse is, and how you gain much more than you ever have to give. I thank Bill and his lovely wife, Dot, for making me a part of their lives, and showing such courage as they met the many challenges of his terminal illness.

Read on and see how nursing can rock your world!

Introduction

Who knew? Providing chocolate cake for a patient at his request can be a nursing skill — especially if that patient is diabetic! That's where the "skilled" part comes in and makes it happen.

I was visiting my patient several days before he passed away when his wife asked him what he wanted for dinner. Sitting with him in his living room finishing the endless documentation that we nurses do, I noticed a gleam come to his eyes and a smile to his face as he thought. Soon he blurted out that he wanted chocolate cake for dinner!

That is what he wanted and that is what he got.

Sometimes putting a smile on a patient's face is the most important function a nurse can provide (though for sure, this man's blood sugar issues got covered in the process of fulfilling his request).

That is what nurses do: meet needs, whatever it takes, if at all humanly and ethically possible. It is no surprise that year after year nursing is recognized as the most trusted profession.

Nursing — yes, nursing — is also the world's best profession! It is not just for women, it is not the lowest paid profession, and it is not drudgework. It is a pathway to your soul and a roadmap to a bright future. If you open your eyes and see, you will know that whatever you give to those you care for will be returned tenfold. Nursing will debunk any thought that society somehow "owes" you an easy living. You will soon learn that it is your privilege to give back to your fellow human beings and that you will benefit hugely by doing so.

Even better is the tremendous variety of ways you can practice nursing. There are so many settings, public and private, civilian and military, all over America and in other countries. Endless opportunities await you. You just have to take that first step and take a good look at what nursing can offer.

Nursing is a profession in which you will experience every emotion known to man. You may go from fear of not performing a nursing task correctly to profound joy in successfully tackling a difficult task. You may go from hating a nursing duty to calmly accepting it as just one minor part of the care you give a patient. You may even go from feeling absolute dislike for a patient to sincere care and appreciation when you realize why the person behaved objectionably. Perhaps they are terribly ill and afraid their healthcare treatment won't produce positive results.

You will go from panic to pride in your work and from an untried skill level to proficiency as you discover that your actions can mean the world to your patients — and to you. Sometimes you are their world, and they need your gift of care.

You'll find many occasions to laugh until you cry. Patients and circumstances often lead to comical moments. You also learn to grieve, recognizing that sometimes you have to release a patient into the next life. You grow to be more human, better fit for society; you become a much more wholesome participant in the world. You learn how to live a positive life. In the words of an old, favorite hymn I've sung all my life, nursing provides those "glimpses of truth thou hast for me." [1]

Nursing teaches you to meet stressful, busy work conditions with a positive attitude, deep-sixing unhelpful worry and anger, because the right attitude is key to improving those taxing conditions and continuing to meet your patients' and coworkers' needs. You learn that it is never okay to put your worries on your patients; their problems are far worse than yours, and you will feel far better prepared to meet your needs when you have successfully helped your patients meet theirs.

Why nursing? Let me show you. Join me in my journey through forty years of enjoying the many friends, rewards, and benefits of nursing — part-time and full-time, civilian and military, from staff nurse to administrator and back, and through the many specialty areas in which I have worked. I wouldn't change any of it. I have learned and greatly benefited from all of it — even the very brief period when I did not work in nursing.

Was it all fun and excitement? Of course not. But there was always a light at the end of the tunnel as well as a paycheck! Let me explain.

Priceless - nursing friends for 38 years and counting!

[1] Clara H. Scott, "Open My Eyes That I May See," 1895

Chapter One

Nursing Can Be a Wild Ride!

Ever since I had a conscious thought, I wanted to be a nurse — an army nurse, after hearing my dad's many stories about his army years. My dad had been an army intelligence officer, and to say he loved military service was putting it mildly. I knew I would, too. I wasn't sure how I knew. I just did.

What I didn't know was that while I became an RN at age twenty-four, I wouldn't become an army nurse until twenty years later. Not until I was forty-four, in 1992, did I receive my commission as a 1LT in the United States Army Reserve Nurse Corps. Stranger yet, another eleven years passed before my only active-duty assignment began. The swinging singles life of World War II in the 1940s in our nation's capitol, described to me by my parents, did not quite work out the same in war-time Washington, D.C. in 2003 when I was fifty-five!

Here is what can happen when you're in the army.

In mid-March of 2003, about two-and-a-half months after my husband, mother, and I had moved to Albuquerque and I was caring for hospice patients in their homes, I received orders to report to Walter Reed Army Medical Center. The duration of the orders was for a year, beginning April 2.

The Iraq War operations had begun in addition

to the War in Afghanistan. My orders were under Operation Noble Eagle in support of those efforts. The orders did not specify where I would serve; they simply stated I was to report to Walter Reed. I had a week or two to put things in order, get packed up, and begin my drive to Walter Reed.

My husband understood, and my mom did mostly — after all, my dad had many decades of army service. But she hated to see me go, as we had just moved her to Albuquerque with us. I have never taken any nursing job without considering my loved ones, and this was no exception. My options, however, were fewer.

I did think about trying to have the orders waived, and I spent some time evaluating my mom's health. She was still independent and still could drive, although not everywhere, and I knew that my husband would be home with her. But he didn't work at the time, and after I left, he would have no car. We had been motor-homing full-time for several months and were down to one vehicle, which would go with me to Washington. This is just not what one does in a marriage of thirty-four years: leave your husband home with your mother and with no car other than hers, and go across country for a year.

But these were not normal times. Our country was involved on two war fronts, and having paid close attention to the threat facing our country since 9/11, I was prepared to serve. I had made sure I had all my military gear, paperwork, and so forth, with me while we were motor-homing so it was readily available.

I even considered bringing my mom with me to Washington, D.C., but we figured she would be trapped if I worked lots of hours. If you're familiar with the traffic around Washington, you can understand that my almost eighty-year-old mother would not be driving much. The flip side, of course, was that it would be up to me to take her wherever she wanted to go. And around Washington, that meant dealing with traffic galore at any time of day or night.

The prospect did not sound appealing to Mom. It certainly was nothing like the fun and excitement she had experienced in Washington during World War II, working for a naval attaché affiliated with the Office of Strategic Services (now the CIA). Back then, she had met and married my dad; this time, she would be waiting for her fifty-five-year-old daughter to get home from work. Not good. And that's provided I stayed at Walter Reed and wasn't sent elsewhere. There were just too many unknowns.

My employer, Presbyterian Hospice, was more than gracious about my leaving so soon after I had joined their team. My patients understood as well. The husband of one of them laughingly said that I would be back in a few months. Our troops would take care of Saddam Hussein and we would all be home in record time. That was not my gut feeling, but my job was simply to go and serve. So with things in order at home, I left for Washington D.C., stopping in Michigan so I could see our son and his wife. I didn't have to worry about visiting our daughter as well, as she lived in the Washington area at the time — something that pleased me greatly!

I figured my husband would not last long without a car of his own, and I was correct. He got a part-time job, and I received a call to forward him power of attorney so he could get a Jeep with my active-duty discount. Wahoo — I was still worth something at home! It just wasn't in the way of being chief cook and bottle washer. But I fully understood that, barring a disaster, I had to obey orders as a soldier. That was my commitment when I accepted my commission in 1992, and it was one I gladly embraced in order to help protect my country from an enemy determined to harm it.

On April 2, I reported to Walter Reed and learned I would be stationed there. Our particular operation, Noble Eagle, provided medical support for Operation Enduring Freedom. I went through a thorough orientation and completed the physical training requirements right away. Before I finished my orientation, I was assigned to work on Ward 57, the orthopedic/trauma ward.

I preferred working nights, and the powers that be were glad to let me as most nurses wanted to work the day shift. I was thrilled to get a choice, and in the army, no less! We worked twelve-hour shifts four nights a week at the start, as the unit was full to overflowing. Operation Iraqi Freedom had started, and already casualties had arrived from Iraq as well as Afghanistan. Walter Reed greatly needed experienced nurses.

The nursing leadership on this ward was second to none. Since the leaders had considerable experience in hands-on nursing, they understood the realities behind our unit's status reports and knew the kind of staffing we needed. What a treat!

Soon I was cast into a charge nurse position on the night shift along with another reservist who had been mobilized at the same time — an excellent, wonderfully warm RN from Wisconsin. What a great friend she became! We were just sorry that we usually ended up working opposite shifts, not together.

After a few weeks living at my post in a hotel, which also housed many family members of the wounded, I got relocated to a furnished apartment in Silver Spring, MD, seven miles away. There I was in Washington, D.C., all by myself, working long hours. What a different picture from my eighteen-year-old vision of a swingin' single life in Washington! At age fifty-five and long married, I certainly wouldn't be partying much. But what followed was one of the most rewarding times of my life. I met and worked with dedicated Army professionals and civilians, developed lasting friendships with fellow workers and patients, and learned a tremendous amount about orthopedic injuries and multi-trauma. At Walter Reed, we had it all, and the wounded kept coming.

By no means was the staff all military; about half was civilian, although some were attached to the army as civilians. There were a lot of agency nurses, many of them recent arrivals from other countries. We used a team staffing model, with RN and LPN civilian and military equivalents as well as nursing aides, or the military's medic level. The military's approach to team staffing has the same strength as the military as a whole. It brings together all levels of healthcare professionals and enhances their ability to perform at their peak, producing positive patient outcomes. In the military, that usually means getting soldiers back on duty! That was certainly the spirit on Ward 57. Staff and patients alike wanted to get the wounded back to work, in whatever capacity that might be. Some of our patients even returned to Iraq, sooner than anyone believed possible and with the resolve of their mission intact — some even with prosthetic legs.

On Ward 57 and on many other wards, the tremendous skill of the different staff levels was a critical aspect of the team. Military LPNs do most of what RNs do in civilian hospitals. They are fully functional nurses. While they cannot perform some of the same legal duties as RNs — doing admission assessments or signing orders, for example — ours possessed the skills that we greatly needed. They started and maintained IVs and IV fluids. They gave medications. They did all manner of treatments, dressing changes, and the like.

Similarly, while the medic level of staff performed what civilians would call nursing aide work, many also had other skills that they performed under RN supervision. Many were trained phlebotomists with lots of field experience. Heck, even a good number of our patients had ample field-medic training and did simple self-treatments whenever possible. Everyone helped, doing whatever they could do to get our patients healed and moving on with their lives.

Most of our wounded were healthy young people in their twenties and thirties who had never been critically sick or in a hospital, let alone experienced traumatic injuries such as amputations. There was definitely a place for a soldier like me with a nursing background of over thirty years. My experience, and I suppose even my gray hair, reassured many of the wounded and their families.

Any caregiver who provided compassionate and quality nursing care day after day had an important role to play. We tried hard to get such conscientious, quality caregivers regularly assigned to Ward 57. The consistency mattered to many of our long-term patients, some of whom were with us for months. Moreover, some patients who got discharged to outpatient status returned for further surgeries or treatment for infection, and they found comfort in having familiar nurses who already knew them.

With wars, injuries follow. The wars in Afghanistan and Iraq were no different in many respects — yet there were some definite differences. Healthcare professionals knew more than those during previous wars such as World War II, Vietnam, and even the Gulf War. Infection control became a huge priority; many of our patients arrived from overseas already with full-blown infections. Different and unknown organisms were causing them, so finding an effective antibiotic treatment was a challenge. Of course, we also encountered old favorites such as methicillin-resistant Staphylococcus aureus, or MRSA. We tested and re-tested.

Ah, the documentation! What the medical profession doesn't have in the way of alphabet soup, the military surely does. A lot of our patient care communication boiled down to letters or numbers. The military's computer system for patient care information and documentation is much the same. It's not exactly user-friendly. Still, I was pleased that our documentation was done via computer. One learns, and I was fortunate to have a great friend who quickly realized that he could help me best by taking over some of the regular administrative needs on the computer, freeing me to care for the patients. I eventually mastered the computer, but I appreciated being able to ease into it while meeting more critical needs. Teamwork — it will work every time.

Several things became immediately clear when I started working on Ward 57. Rank mattered little in prioritizing the care we gave to all. Every patient was given the same courtesies of being addressed by their rank and treated with respect. And those with the most critical needs received the promptest attention and the available staff member best trained to meet a given need.

Some of us from the civilian side even let our patients call us by our given names. In the middle of the night, which was when we usually got in transports from Landstuhl, Germany, it just did not seem necessary to introduce myself as Captain Burch. Sylvia Burch would do fine. The arrivals were tired, and I was probably tired too, and wanting them to get some rest before the morning hullabaloo. And after all, what's in a name? So I answered to anything. Yet however wounded, exhausted, and in pain most of the soldiers were, they adhered to their usual courtesies. So mostly I was Ma'am.

Our night staff was pretty darned adept at getting our new soldiers rapidly admitted, meeting their needs, and then leaving them alone to sleep as much as possible. No frills — just precise, immediately needed care. Even though the flight crews did a super job of ensuring adequate comfort, the time spent on transport aircraft was never easy for the injured, so they arrived exhausted and usually in pain. Providing pain relief, wound care, and then sleep were the priorities we met.

Layers of dirt and grime covered our arrivals. We never fussed about it. The soldiers were horrified at their own uncleanliness, and they understood that the layers of filth harbored infectious organisms. They would never have presented to a hospital ward as anything but clean, shaved and appropriately dressed.

Most were also severely dehydrated. In the early days of the Iraq War, water supplies were limited in some areas, and with injury, hospitalization, transport, infection, and blood loss, the soldiers became even more dehydrated.

Some arrived without any personal belongings, adding to their sense of loss. They knew their role and mission as a soldier, but as wounded warriors they were out of their familiar norm. Two young arrivals from Iraq who were able to walk onto our ward stood at attention when they presented, expecting a formation! These men and women deserved our utmost respect and the best care we could deliver.

Many of our soldiers had not seen their loved ones for months, and some for well over a year. Family members naturally wanted to stay as long as they could with their loved ones, and many did not understand why they could not be there 24/7. Civilian hospitals make accommodations for visitors to stay, but the military hospitals were a different story. Historically, visiting hours were strictly adhered to. But times, they were a-changin', and Walter Reed changed with them with a little help from some of us nurses. I believe the majority of the military staff members were okay with family members staying around the clock. A few were a tough sell, but they got over it. And why not? Ninety-nine percent of the time, family members were not only supportive of their loved ones but also very helpful. Many nursing care needs are greatly aided by a helping hand, and the care we delivered at Walter Reed was no exception.

Jessica Lynch, the sweet young lady who had been taken by the Iraqis briefly and then rescued, made our ward famous by the media hype that hounded her. When asked if I wanted to help her team of caregivers, I hedged a bit, as she already had a full component of staff dedicated to her care. The extra attention was nothing Jessica would have asked for; that is just the way it is with any POW. But there were many more patients on the ward who also needed nursing care, and they and their families noticed that there was always a lot of action around Jessica's room. So while her presence was supposed to be kept secret early on, it didn't take a rocket scientist to figure out that she was there.

I opted to work with the rest of the patients and felt that decision helped me get the overall picture of their needs quickly. We nurses made sure all felt they were getting the care they needed. Nurses do that well: we look out for all.

Many of our patients have moved on with their lives and into productive work since their stays on Ward 57, including Jessica Lynch, who graduated from college in West Virginia and has done well for herself. Such success stories are our greatest reward for the long hours of patient care we were privileged to give the wounded.

I chose to work nights at Walter Reed for the same reason I have always worked nights. Fewer people are on duty, and they are all there to help deliver patient care. During the day, there are always a lot more bodies around, but not all of them are direct caregivers. Walter Reed had even more non-caregivers about, including a lot of well-meaning, distinguished visitors who came to see our patients almost daily. We also had not only a variety of medical providers, but of personnel management players who had to meet with active-duty patients. Soldiers often spoke of all the paperwork they had to do in addition to their treatments. Infection control specialists and psychiatrists were some of the first specialists our patients saw besides their surgeons. Our wounded had a full complement of care and then some.

We nurses strove to work around visitors in order to provide necessary patient care in a timely manner. We had visitors from the Veterans Administration, Red Cross, and many other organizations, all providing helpful services to our patients and families. Scores of veterans came to support the wounded warriors.

We even had an embedded journalist at one point. That was a new experience, and not one I'd care to repeat unless they get their story right. The one that eventually hit the news reported that one of our finest and most dedicated lieutenants had hassled one of the wounded about his identification when he was due to fly home. In fact, the Lieutenant was trying to ensure that when the soldier got to the airport, he would have the proper identification to board his flight and not be turned away. Working as hard as we were at that point, the spin on that story did not sit well with us. Our patients knew who had their back, though.

It was normally quieter at night, and our shift began by preparing our patients to get some sleep. Mornings started very early for them. The surgical teams made their rounds between 4:30 and 5:30 a.m., going room-to-room doing dressing changes and the like. This was often a rude awakening for the soldiers, but they put up with it, and then went right back to sleep. Helping them to get several hours of rest met a need that was every bit as important as medications, treatments, and surgeries. We nurses were determined to get it right for our soldiers: the whole gamut of care and nothing less.

Getting a moment's pause and laugh during the night shift.

The patients attended an incredible number of appointments! They had personnel issues, dental appointments, vaccinations, and haircuts, if they could get off the ward. They had to see this specialist or that one. They had physical therapy, occupational therapy, or both. In short, these wounded warriors were on the go all the time, especially during the day. It's amazing that the day shift could get any care done! By nighttime, the soldiers were exhausted and put up little argument about turning off the lights. We made sure they received all their medications and that their treatments were done, their pain pumps were filled, and in short, that as many of their care needs as possible got met before ten o'clock so they could get some rest.

A few of our distinguished visitors came in the evening. General Myers, then Chairman of the Joint Chiefs of Staff, and his wife often came, usually along with the Assistant Secretary of Defense, Paul Wolfowitz. They were among my favorite visitors; they always listened attentively to the soldiers express their needs and worked with the staff to meet those needs. Mrs. Myers always came with homemade cookies, which was another hit!

The soldiers definitely had their favorite visitors too. Cute female country singers were always a hit with the men. If their injuries didn't make them swoon, a beautiful young talent like Chely Wright surely could do the trick when she brought her guitar and sat down in patient rooms to sing.

The Incredible Hulk was another favorite visitor. He had a great time joking with the soldiers and staff. Visitors like the Hulk helped lighten the heavy loads borne by the wounded in returning to health. The staff had fun with these visitors too. Michael Jordan, Gary Sinise Winonah Judd, and many others came to pay their respects and left knowing that their visits were much appreciated.

Before a visitor came, the patients were always asked if they wanted to see that particular visitor. They did not have to see anyone they didn't wish to see. We made a list of the patients who would accept a visitor, and that's what we abided by with any visitor, even President Bush.

My friend Jim Mayer from the Veterans Administration, another favorite, became known as the "Milkshake Man," as he always stopped at McDonald's and got milkshakes for any soldiers who wanted them. He often brought a friend or two to help him bring even more milkshakes. You have no idea what those milkshakes meant to the wounded soldiers — they were so grateful. Many who had served in the deserts and taxing terrain of Iraq and Afghanistan had not enjoyed such a simple pleasure as a milkshake for as long as a year. The wounded counted Jim a great friend as he did so much for them in keeping their spirits up, organizing outings, and many other Veteran services. If ever a person had a heart for service, it was Jim, and our patients knew that. Jim was also a Vietnam Veteran. He was among the many Vietnam veterans who came from all over the country to show our wounded outstanding support, some of the best they received.

Jim's contributions to our newest veterans did not end with milkshakes. He also teamed up with his great friend, Hal Koster, who was also a Vietnam Veteran, to provide free steak dinners for the wounded and their family members. Hal was co-owner of Fran O'Brien's Stadium Steakhouse in downtown Washington, D.C. In October of 2003, he began what became a great tradition for the wounded and their family members, hosting steak dinners every Friday night. Not everyone could get their physician's approval to attend, but if they could go, they did, often with a family member.

Friday night dinner at Fran O'Brien's.

Staff members with a car, like me, could volunteer to bring a few soldiers. My Saturn station wagon could hold a few soldiers and their equipment. Many of our wounded were amputees, so crutches, wheelchairs, and such were likely to be part of the package. I became expert at taking apart wheelchairs to fit them in my car, but the soldiers themselves were awesome at getting out of the car, hopping around to the back, removing their equipment, and putting it together for themselves. One thing about these warriors: if they could do something for themselves, they did, consistently.

They were simply the best of America. They had fun when they could, but they also endured the ever-present pain and miseries of healing from traumatic injuries. They made fun of themselves, ragged on each other mercilessly, and ensured that they all got out together whenever possible. My head nurse arranged my schedule so I could provide rides to many events, and these wonderful human beings worried about me going back to my apartment late at night after I returned them to Walter Reed. They reminded me that Washington, D.C., could be a dangerous place — as if where they had recently come from was a picnic! I even had to call one of them when I got home. Soldiers are like that: they look out for each other.

The free dinners for the soldiers took a turn in 2006, I learned. Fran O'Brien's lost its lease at the Hilton downtown and had to move their equipment out. A few organizations and private donors contributed to the foundation that Hal Koster had established in 2005, the Aleethia Foundation, in order to keep the dinner tradition going for the soldiers and marines at Walter Reed and the National Naval Medical Center. The patients dined at different restaurants as Hal and others found the resources to keep the dinners running.

Hal would never mention the recognition he has received, but I will. He is the recipient of several awards for his services to these newest veterans and their families, including the Department of Defense Distinguished Public Service Award in October 2004. President George W. Bush, Secretary of Defense Donald Rumsfeld, and many others have written him letters of appreciation.

Hal made light of his twenty-four months in Vietnam as a gunship crew chief with the 174th Assault Helicopter Company. He knew how to serve and he continues to serve. People like Hal Koster and Jim Mayer, who give their best in practical ways on behalf of our troops, are true heroes. They are certainly my heroes.

Among our other many visitors, I had the privilege of meeting President George W. Bush and First Lady Laura Bush and seeing them make the rounds with the patients. The soldiers greatly appreciated the visit from their Commander in Chief. The whole hospital turned upside down in preparation, but it was worth it to see the joy not only on the soldiers' faces but also on the President's and Mrs. Bush's. Going from soldier to soldier, they heard a little of each person's story. President Bush recognized not only his ability to send men and women to war, but also the responsibility of that power. He felt deep anguish for every life changed by injuries, and he shared the sorrow of families grieving the loss of beloved soldiers. I saw the sincerity of those feelings in President and Mrs. Bush. A few of the wounded did not wish to see the President, and their wishes were honored. Far more, however, wanted to tell their commander of their support. I saw how touched the President was when a soldier told him, "We're praying for you, Mr. President."

President Bush made time to pray with them.

If I never see a wound vacuum again, that will be just fine with me. I saw plenty of them during my mobilization. And they weren't the only kind of equipment that I met up with daily. There were IV pumps, pain pumps, suction machines, feeding tube machines, and more.

The equipment doesn't always work well, and it doesn't always fail one piece at a time, either.

On any given night, you could find nurses running from room to room answering beeps from machines that needed a fix. Most of the patients grew accustomed to the sound and often kept sleeping, but I don't think we staff ever got used to those raucous beeps.

The computer system could go down too. Sometimes we had warnings, sometimes not. Sometimes we had to finish all our documentation at the last moment when the system finally came back up at the end of our shift. That end-of-the-shift thing... if something could go wrong then, or if multiple needs could suddenly present, they did. We seemed to get out later and later all the time, only to come back in a few more hours. One did not arrive late for a shift, and being on time meant showing up at least a half-hour early. Sleep was a gift not often received in full measure.

As with any military duty, there were meetings to attend, mandatory educational in-services, and volunteer activities that took up a lot of non-working days. And let's not forget training for physical testing! Somehow I found the energy to run my two miles a couple times a week and do the mandatory sit-ups and push-ups. I figured that at my age, if I didn't maintain some degree of regular exercise, I could meet a bad end during the actual testing.

One thing I did not do was sign up to train for a marathon when a young lieutenant asked me to. I told her I was thinking of starting a Two Miles and Not One Step More Club — at which poin another lieutenant said, "Hey, Captain Burch, I'll be your vice president!" This young lady could easily beat out her competition in a two-mile run, but evidently she didn't like running. I always felt better after I ran, but enough was enough. I passed my PT testing and life was good. And I kept my marathons to providing patient care.

You learn a lot when you get sucked into the hyperactivity of a busy trauma surgery ward. You learn efficiencies you've never dreamed of. You find out that each caregiver has his or her own strengths, and you had better learn to work with them all.

While most of our patients came from Iraq or Afghanistan, not all were active-duty. Occasionally a veteran, a non-combat soldier, or a spouse managed to get a slot for a knee replacement or some such. One colonel fell off a ladder on the third story of his house while trying to assist a satellite dish installer. He had a lot of broken bones and soft tissue injuries, but he was a good sport throughout his stay. I finally got around to asking him why he thought he had to help the installer, and I could have scripted his answer: he just wanted to help. That's a soldier for ya! When I came back to Walter Reed around the holidays of 2005 and 2006, this same man came up to the ward to say hello to anyone working there who had cared for him. What a change a year-plus of healing can make!

Another amazingly heroic colonel came to Ward 57 to have surgical excisions made at the lower end of his spinal cord, into his sacrum, for a vicious form of cancer. He had several surgeries and remissions over the two to three years that I knew him, along with several courses of chemotherapy. I drove him back to his home when he was discharged from one of his stays for chemo. His wife was extremely sick and could not pick him up, nor did she want her illness to compromise his decreased ability to fight infection. He has since lost his battle with his disease, but he and his brave family have left me a memory that I cherish.

Witnessing the strength of some military families was an experience I will never forget. One of my patients had a battle buddy who was in ICU, comatose, with severe head trauma and several other injuries. The reports my patient got from his buddy's family grew increasingly somber, and so did my patient's demeanor. It did not look like his friend would make it.

Finally the injured soldier's wife came up to tell my patient that her husband was dying. She thought my patient would like to say good-bye. He was undone, but he was also grateful to have the opportunity, and he asked me if I would take him to the ICU. After securing an order to do so from his surgeon, I brought him down, and he said good-bye to his buddy.

Afterward, back on Ward 57, he and I sat and watched the sun come up and talked about what a new day could bring.

In my view, the soldiers and marines who were in the fight knew they could be injured. Many seemed prepared to fight any battle for recovery that they had to fight. One man told me that not seeing his little girls grow up to be women would be the worst thing that could happen to him. He didn't seem to mind that he was minus a leg. In fact, he was one of the best wheelchair racers on our ward. He and another soldier always tried to beat each other to the elevator when they were leaving the floor. They healed quickly, those two — I think because of the extra adrenalin they pumped up with their races!

Another man told me that he feared a brain injury that would leave him comatose. He was afraid that his wife would not let him go and he would have to live, if you could call it that, in a coma.

But the worst thing that these brave souls endured was the loss of a buddy or fellow soldier. We nurses listened to lots of such stories, when and if the soldiers were ready to share them. We prayed with those who asked us to. We tried to always be in touch with the needs — voiced or unvoiced — of the soldiers, who also received great support from mental health and spiritual providers. Meeting our patients' spiritual and emotional support seemed to help in their recoveries as much as the medical treatments we delivered hour after hour, day after day.

Most of the wounded were active duty soldiers, reservists, guard soldiers, or others in the eighteen- to thirty-five-year-old range. A few, however, were in their fifties, and I even cared for a sixty-five-year-old sergeant with a badly broken elbow. I thanked him for being the one patient on the ward who was older than I was, and eventually I asked why he was over in Iraq getting his elbow shot up at his age. He shrugged. He had high-value, specialized abilities as a truck mechanic, so the army had called him back to serve in the Gulf War and now Iraq. He and his wife worked in a factory out west, and he planned to go back there, injury or not, along with his wife.

Most nurses would not think of physical therapy as Comedy Central, but that's the way it struck me. When I went down to see how a patient was faring with his or her therapy, I often had a lot of laughs. The soldiers and veterans — male and female, young and old — would harass each other, compete with each other, and generally badmouth anyone who slacked in their efforts. It was great camaraderie that often carried back to the ward — soldiers helping other soldiers and marines at its best. A patient's branch of service didn't matter. Perhaps the first marine or two who came to the ward felt a bit like an outsider, but that didn't last. All were in it together — soldier, sailor, and airman; male and female; old and young; veterans from other conflicts; even the occasional injured civilian or media representative — everyone was in the fight, rooting for one another.

I got to practice a wide variety of nursing skills while at Walter Reed. There was an overabundance of intravenous therapy, IV starts and restarts, more permanent IV line management, medications of every sort, wound vacs, dressing changes, and numerous pain pumps to keep up with. We wanted to keep our patients as comfortable as possible, and with multi-trauma, that was a challenge. One of my patients' dad once commented that the wounded treated Percocet, a painkiller, like candy. We did hand out a lot of Percocet, especially while weaning a patient from IV pain medication.

Tubes of all sorts inserted in our patients required strict attention to placement and functionality. With orthopedic trauma, the potential for developing blood clots or infections was always a concern, so we carefully watched vital signs and wounds. We treated and cured some tenacious infections, joint infections being among the worst; we were exceedingly careful with dressing changes and all infection-prevention measures. Yet too often, soldiers discharged as outpatients returned due to infection. So we spent a lot of time teaching our patients how to safeguard against infection, and we reinforced those teachings consistently.

We even did some case management. My reservist friend Cindy and I convinced our head nurse to let us manage a team of patients, overseeing their treatments and modifying them when a change in a patient's condition required it. I took one side of the ward and Cindy took the other. We had to be flexible, as patients often got moved when new infections were diagnosed. We could have two with the same infectious organism room together, but not two patients with different infections. We did not want any crossover infections. I doubt the infectious disease specialists ever rested; they probably are still hard at work at Walter Reed.

My Walter Reed experience utilized every bit

of training and experience I had ever had in nursing, except for the work of delivering babies. It also added a few new skills and the time to perfect them.

Mishaps occur in every hospital. Our staff coped with them all quite well at Walter Reed. Not all our patients needed IV fluids going all the time, but they did receive IV antibiotics at consistent intervals around the clock. We disturbed our patients as little as possible at night, hooking up their IV antibiotics, running them in for as long as necessary, then disconnecting the IV line while maintaining the IV site in the patient's arm for the next round.

One night an emergency light came on in an amputation patient's room, and I ran in to see blood sprayed from one end of the room to the other and pooling by the man's remaining foot as he stood in the bathroom on one leg. He looked fine, but the room did not. While hopping to the bathroom waving his arms about for balance, he had ripped out his running IV and splattered blood all over the place. In my horror at the scene, all I could say was, "Jesus Christ in the mountains, Brian, it looks like something from Silence of the Lambs in here!" Very unprofessional, of course, but my patient understood — and offered to help me clean up. That too is a soldier for ya.

Between the clean up, patch up, IV restart, and so forth, such incidents take time to fix, but they seldom happen twice with the same patient. There are other incidents, of course. One sergeant got tired of hearing the soldier in the next room make a fuss. He went in and told the man in no uncertain terms that his behavior was inappropriate for a soldier and he had better button it up and be respectful. Since the ward was enjoying an otherwise quiet moment, we could hear the sergeant giving his fellow trooper holy hell in a well-controlled but no-nonsense, angry voice. When he was finished, the sergeant came out and advised me of his activity, fully expecting to be reported. I told him I had heard nothing. Soldiers take care of soldiers.

One night, an army captain by the name of David Rozelle was admitted to our ward minus a foot he had lost in Iraq. He was in great spirits, didn't seem at all tired, and told me the only thing I needed to do for him was help him shower as his parents would be there in the morning. That was in another few hours. He understood that I had to do a few other things, ask a few questions, at least roughly get him admitted and into the system, but cleanliness was topmost on his mind. He was not about to have his parents see him unshaven and unclean after so much time apart. It was enough for them to bear that he came home without a foot.

He got his shower, and so did I by the time I had helped him. I was probably as wet as he was. Thankfully, he was capable of shaving on his own once I got him the supplies, as shaving men was never my forte. He was spit-and-polish clean, with a fresh dressing on his leg courtesy of his surgeon, when his folks arrived.

David had another mission, and that was to get back to Colorado to see the birth of his first child. His wife could not come to Walter Reed as she was almost nine months pregnant. This weighed on David's mind during his brief stay at Walter Reed, and he returned to Colorado in time for the birth. I am sure that meant the world to him and his wife. However, as he later recalled in a book he wrote, he returned too soon. Like all wounded soldiers, he needed time at Walter Reed to come down from his experience in Iraq, get the necessary surgeries, treatments, and consultations, and receive the appropriate care to get through the hurdles and on with the rest of his life.

David, being one smart man, came out of the funk he sank into briefly in Colorado and is still serving in the Army. He was the first amputee veteran of Operation Iraqi Freedom to return to Iraq, not just once but twice. David recalled his experience in a fabulous book titled *Back In*

Action.

I had been at Walter Reed about a year when I was chosen as the nurse to go with the first-ever Walter Reed contingent to the Disabled Veterans Winter Sports Clinic at Snowmass, Colorado. I was a tremendous week of fun and camaraderie with veterans of wars from World War II on up participating in the various sports activities as well as some fun social ones. The event had a medical clinic staffed by nurses and doctors from various VA facilities to treat minor injuries, illnesses, and other medical needs. We took shifts in the clinic, chose certain sports events to help with, and had a great time. Many of our recently wounded Iraq and Afghanistan veterans came with us, and they enjoyed the Winter Sports Clinic to the max. With several surgeons, a therapist, and an orthotics specialist from Walter Reed on board, we were equipped to help with medical treatment of many kinds. During our shifts at the medical clinic, we got to work with other providers who had been caring for veterans for a long time, and we gained from their insights into wounded veteran care.

It was wonderful to see the older vets receive the newer vets so warmly. The degree of activity most of the veterans could do — skiing downhill, skating, sledding, and more — was simply amazing. One legally blind gentleman in his eighties told me he'd keep on doing downhill skiing as long as someone would take him on a tether! And the unforgettable Dana Bowman put on an astonishing performance, jumping out of an airplane with skis on his two prosthetic legs, landing on the hillside, and then skiing downhill. Superb! Dana had been a member of the army's Golden Knights parachute team prior to losing his legs in an accident. That did not stop him. He made his first jump after his accident five months later and even reenlisted in the army. In the motivational speeches he gives all over the country, Dana speaks not about disability but about ability. He is a role model for wounded vets as well as many other amputees.

I was thrilled to be invited back to the Winter Sports Clinic the next year as well, even though I was then off active duty. It was a joy to participate with old friends and new ones as well.

The events planned for our wounded warriors continue today, and I am grateful. I certainly never expected anything like the variety of events that occurred when I was at Walter Reed those first fifteen months of the Iraq War. Going in a motorcade down to the Capitol and Washington Mall to see a season opening NFL event was a winner. The soldiers were happy about seeing Britney Spears perform, but I can't say we could even hear her voice. I guess she was singing, but I'm not sure the soldiers cared. They were impressed with her costume, and I doubt they would have minded if she sang off-key as long as they could look at her!

Our motorcade went through all the traffic lights as well, so we got to wave at the passersby who were cheering for our troops. It was quite an honor to be escorted by White House motorcade police. One of our staff who was a native of Washington, D.C. was in absolute awe. She had never been in such a motorcade before, surrounded by the Capitol police. She just couldn't believe that she was stopping traffic!

I cannot say enough about the fine army surgeons who treated our wounded. Our soldiers received not only the best surgical and medical treatment ever offered to war wounded, but they received compassionate treatment as well.

Orthopedic surgeons do not routinely release patients with recent surgically treated wounds, or who are hooked up to a wound vac or other appliance, to the outside world. The surgeons want to avoid any risk of infection or other complications.

However, for the mental health of our patients and to free them from worrying about wound healing, our surgeons allowed many to leave Walter Reed for special events. We all knew the risks, but we also knew the visible benefits to our wounded in allowing them some activities outside the hospital. To be sure, we nurses went with our patients, often carrying their medications and sometimes even dressing supplies. We were more than willing to go the extra mile to witness the joy such events brought to our troops. I doubt I could prove it, but I highly suspect such outings sped their healing.

I would like to give a special shout-out to my friend Ric, one of the best-ever nurses with whom I have worked. Ric is an LPN. mentioned him earlier as the great friend who took over many of my computer-related duties as a charge nurse when I first came to Walter Reed. Ric had the uncanny ability to know what was going on all over the ward — where the hot spots were and who needed help and when. His broad diversity of experience meant he could be relied on to take care of any of our patients. He worked well with all the staff, and his competence earned their respect. Ric ensured that I really did know what I was doing on the computer, and he helped in other ways that went far beyond what we nurses were taught in training.

Ric even supplied me with an old printer of his. That came in handy since I was finishing my doctoral dissertation while on active duty. He introduced me to Five Guys, too, although I'm not sure I should thank him for that. Calories, calories!

Ric also went antiquing with me. He knew most of the great places around the D.C. area in which to shop. Even better, Ric's friend, Jon, worked at Starbucks. Oh, what a great bonus for a coffeeholic such as I! Jon wasn't a nurse, but he surely understood nurses, and I could get a caffeine buzz just listening to him talk about the various blends of coffee. Heaven!

My fellow reservist, Cindy, went home after her year of service. Both of us were asked to extend another three months, but Cindy had four growing boys at home, so she got to go home after a year. I stayed for another three months after spending a week at our home in New Mexico. It was difficult to get on the plane back to Washington, D.C., but I did and finished out my orders. I was almost done when along came our first grandchild, almost six weeks early. So I was not yet to go home to my husband and mom. I went to Michigan to help our son and his wife with their new five-pound son. I helped feed him in those wee hours of the night when I was used to working so his parents could get some sleep. From orthopedic trauma to premature newborn care — that's a nurse's world!

Chapter Two

How It All Started

I didn't get from childhood dreams to Walter Reed without a lot of nursing experience and education in between. I am quite sure I must have "nursed" my dolls in my childhood, and I tried to take care of my older brother, too — although usually it was the opposite, with him looking out for me.

Not always, though. Once, while my brother and I were fighting, he flipped me over his head onto the basement floor. I remember my head hitting the hard tile floor. I was stunned, but that didn't stop me. Picking myself up, I bit him on the shoulder.

I don't think I tended to my brother that time. But I do remembering worrying that his shoulder would be okay — one of my early concerns to promote wound healing! It made me forget that my head hurt.

Nursing is like that: you forget your own concerns as you help others deal with theirs.

I learned a lot about being a nurse and wanting to be a nurse from my routine visits to the doctor's office. Of course, maybe the wanting part was partly because I would rather have been the nurse giving the shot than the kid taking it!

Our mother was a champ at getting my brother and me used to our doctor visits, though. As we sat in the waiting room, hearing cries and screams issuing from the inner sanctum, our mother would look at us calmly and say, "You won't be doing that. You're not going to cry." Then she would calmly go back to reading her magazine, signaling that we were to do the same. Of course, I was thinking, "Really? I'm not going to cry? Then what's with that kid who IS howling like a banshee in there?" I guessed it was just because he or she didn't have a mother like mine to rule out such a response.

Years later, I would cheerfully repeat the same line to my labor patients: "Heck no, you're not going to scream or cry." I had learned from my mother's approach, and it almost always worked, even when I got those "Oh, really?" looks. When that technique didn't work, there were other options, mainly of the pain medication or epidural variety. Like my mom, I would stay right there to reinforce my statement, helping to relieve pain and other unpleasant symptoms any way I could. Yet also like my mom, I knew that sometimes a person just has to go through the treatment, pain or no pain. Nursing offers the great privilege of providing much-needed support that helps patients along every step of the way.

At age thirteen, I was diagnosed with epilepsy after having several grand mal seizures. Coming from out of nowhere, the seizures left me shell-shocked. To say I was horrified in no way describes my feelings. I was already experiencing the usual changes and feelings teens go through, and now this! Was I going to be liked? Popular? Have a boyfriend? Be able to drive a car?

I had several seizures over eight months until the medication I was taking became therapeutic and I stabilized. Then the seizures disappeared for a few years. My mother watched me like a hawk, making sure I took my medication on time, which is very important in controlling seizures. She was a superb nurse, I realized several years later.

Did I thank my mom for her tremendous care and concern? No. I resented her close vigilance and disliked that my condition seemed to feed her already worrying nature. I wanted to be free to do all the things my peers were doing, including taking swimming class in gym, something that school rules and my neurologist would not allow. It was another lesson learned and recalled many times during my nursing life when faced with patients who were not thrilled with their doctor's or nurse's advice or with treatment specifics. You just explain fully, give options when possible, and otherwise do what you have to do.

I didn't care much for my neurologist at the time either. I was not fond of being told I could not do the things I wanted to do, and I felt left out. However, I did note that he always stayed calm talking with me and my mom, who was always with me at my doctor visits, even when my dad also came. The neurologist never spoke only to my mom while ignoring me — he spoke to both of us, and that stuck with me, a lesson well learned: Never speak around a patient. Speak to them as well as their significant family members. If a patient cannot understand what you are saying, keep information as simple and appropriate as possible. Today, with plenty of age-appropriate training, medical professionals learn early not to leave teens out of their own treatment planning, and they anticipate responses such as fear and resentment. There is training for all nursing needs!

Once my medication control was accomplished, I was seizure-free for several years. I took my medication faithfully and did follow-up visits with the neurologist. Then at age eighteen, when I was a senior in high school and accepted at both the University of Michigan and Michigan State University, I went on a low- or non-carbohydrate diet known as the Air Force Diet and subsequently experienced what would be my last seizure. It occurred at school. I was horrified, shocked, miserably angry, and totally embarrassed, for a grand mal seizure often resulted in loss of bladder control — not a desirable scenario for a peer-conscious teenager.

I was also scared. What would happen if I had a seizure while caring for a patient and harmed the patient? Such forebodings were far worse than any resentment I felt toward my parents for the restrictions they had placed on me, which included not allowing me to drive.

The seizure led me to switch my college plans. Rather than pursue Registered Nursing at the University of Michigan in Ann Arbor, I decided to study political science at Michigan State University in East Lansing. My brother was already there, running for MSU on a track scholarship, so I'd have many super track meets to attend! And with a degree in political science, I could go to Washington, D.C., and work for some government or military organization as my parents had done during World War II. What wasn't to romanticize for a young girl like I was! Being part of a cause in the nation's capitol appealed to me. And Washington was where my parents met and married. Maybe something good like that might happen to me as well. But I think my primary motive was that no one would know me there — including my history with seizures.

To an eighteen-year-old, that was a big advantage. Being totally new to a scene would solve all my identity issues, or so I thought; and whatever popularity I gained would not be clouded by people feeling sorry for me because I had seizures.

But living and working in Washington after graduating from MSU never happened, and for a very good reason. After my first year at MSU, I met Jim, my husband, who was attending General Motors Institute (now Kettering University) and was also in the East Lansing area working at the Oldsmobile plants. He would spend six weeks going to school in Flint, then work for six weeks in Lansing — six weeks at one, six weeks at the other, back and forth. Jim finished his bachelor's program on the five year target, but I hurried through my education at MSU, going to summer school so I could stay closer to him, and graduated in three years.

We got married and stayed in the Lansing, Michigan, area after graduation, as my husband was now a full-fledged General Motors engineer with a real job. There weren't a lot of jobs nearby that called for a political science major. Lansing was certainly not the capitol I had envisioned working in for a swingin' single's life! Of course, I was no longer single, and I was fully occupied trying to find my very first job out of college, not to mention learning how to be married.

At age twenty-one, I had a ring on my finger and a degree in hand, but not a clue what to do with that degree. I ended up taking the first job I was offered and worked at General Motors Acceptance Corporation (GMAC) for a year. Being in the automotive credit business was not my cup of tea! I spent most of that time applying for and getting accepted into Lansing Community College's Registered Nursing program. The love of my life, poor man, was about to put me through the first of three more degree programs. My dad had warned my husband-to-be that I wanted to own a horse some day, but Jim had not realized that ongoing education would be a factor. He was okay with this decision, though, telling me that he had always wanted to marry a nurse. The important people in my life sometimes know what I am going to do before I do it!

Oh, the fun of it — going back to school a year after rushing through my bachelor's degree! But within the first month of nursing school, I knew that nursing was indeed my life's calling. It wasn't so much that I found nursing; rather, I think nursing found me and my need to be of service. I still feel the same today. I am sure it helped that I was in a first-rate associate degree program with excellent, well-trained nurse professors and great clinical mentors. We students were in hospitals or nursing homes right from the start. I might only say hello to a patient and take a medical history, but nevertheless I was walking into the rooms of patients, introducing myself as a nursing student, and telling them what I would be doing for or with them.

It was wonderful! I must have drawn the long straw, as I had great luck with patients reacting positively. Some of my classmates were not so lucky, learning sooner than later that not everyone was going to think nurses were the next best thing to spun sugar when we came in their room to do an assessment or treatment. Horror of horrors, some patients didn't even want a bath! We lost several students from our nursing program after the first month of classes, perhaps even earlier. The rest of us just forged on, digging into the nitty-gritty of nursing from the start even though classes and studying took up much of our days.

Nursing school will remain one of the highlights of my life. It required a lot of studying, and my husband and mother-in-law expected that I would be an A student. After all, I was well prepared and eager to be a nurse. That was certainly another "Really?" moment!

Fortunately, since my bachelor's degree had been in a social science, many of my previous classes filled course requirements, enabling me to do a condensed two-year stint that was mostly nursing. What a blessing — jumping directly into medical-surgical nursing, pediatrics, mother-baby nursing, and the like, and always spending plenty of time in clinical settings!

I gained several close friends with whom I studied often and learned a lot. We never forgot my husband in our study sessions, which were usually at night when he was home. With their kids in bed, my friends were free to come to my house, and we had plenty of requests for Jim. Popcorn, please. And would he kindly keep the soda and coffee flowing, so we didn't have to break away from learning the fine points of the various body systems, which we had to know inside and out — literally. Somehow it seemed easier to verbally diagram the flow of blood through the heart and great vessels when we were chomping on handfuls of popcorn!

I believe the reason why the four of us who studied together usually ended up at my house is because I had great help from Jim and no kids to interfere or ask us questions about body systems that we probably could not have answered well at that point. Neither would we have wanted to awaken sleeping children when we got to shrieking with laughter. We learned, though, because of each other; we were individually motivated, with strong wills to excel.

The summer between my two years of concentrated nursing study, I served as a nursing extern at Sparrow Hospital in Lansing. I loved it! I worked eight-hour nights on an orthopedic/general surgery floor with seasoned LPNs and RNs. I learned from all of them. One of the best nurses and on-the-job educators was an LPN; there was not much about nursing care that she did not know. Working with her, and with many LPNs since, instilled respect in me for their nursing expertise. Consequently, I have never taken kindly to denigration of LPNs by RNs, as if LPNs are lesser entities. Throughout my nursing life, I have found professionalism at all levels of caregiving. The truly awesome healthcare workers I have worked with have ranged from a thorough and devoted housekeeper/companion to doctoral-prepared nurses. It's the attitude that counts, and commitment to excellence in service.

The funniest part of my summer nursing experience was the carefully structured report I always received from the Nursing Extern I, whose patients I took over at 11:00 p.m. She always promptly reminded me to sign my name as Nursing Extern II, since I was an associate degree RN student, not a bachelor's degree RN student. I must have forgotten that distinction once or twice, but I certainly heard about it many a time! I often wondered what she thought I did with these patients after she left — whether I in some way ruined them, since I was not a Nursing Extern I. I don't recall that the patients complained!

I quickly realized that such minor distinctions and self-assessments of superiority had no place in the teamwork needed on a busy surgical unit — or any other floor, for that matter. There are different levels of care appropriate to the different levels of nursing preparedness, certainly, and nurses learn them and abide by job descriptions and requirements. But we also learn that experience has its place.

The knowledge gained from practicing as a nurse extern was priceless. I learned from my patients as well as my nursing mentors on the floor and gradually worked my way up to higher acuity patient loads as my experience grew. Sparrow Hospital had the best nursing system, I felt, and later years with other nurse staffing systems, not to mention the team-leading semester I had in my second year of nursing school, reinforced that opinion. At Sparrow, you were given a set of patients whose acuity met your skills, and you did everything for them;

there were no nursing aides — just RNs and LPNs, and a few externs now and then. You knew what was going on with your patients. You had to, as there was no one else to make up for any lack of care on your part until the next shift started. And expecting them to complete your undone work was a non-starter. Respect for each other's work was a necessity. You left your patients in the best shape possible if you wanted to earn the respect of your peers and your patients' validation that you had met their needs.

My experience as an extern gave me an education in pain management. I sometimes got the report that a patient had asked for a pain medication, but "they didn't really need it yet, so I didn't give it." You can imagine what happens when such a request gets ignored: you find a patient in a lot of pain and very upset. I learned that a patient's pain is what they describe, not what you think. You give pain medication as ordered or work with the doctor to change it up if it is not working for the patient. It is a lot more difficult to resolve a patient's pain if you have to catch up to it.

Reasonable concerns about what a patient reports can be dealt with, but simply withholding what is available when a patient presents with pain is not acceptable — ever. Disrespecting a patient's observations of their pain or other symptoms probably has more to do with a nurse's laziness or control issues than with reality. Moreover, drug addiction does not result from pain medication received in the hospital, and I could educate my patients on that score if they were afraid to take a pain medication for that reason.

I learned many practical things about patient care at Sparrow. For instance...

- A nursing cap and an overhead traction setup do not work well together. My nursing cap never returned to my head after I made that discovery.
- Never awaken a combat veteran by lightly tapping them on the shoulder or calling their name while standing next to their bed. They come up swinging.
- Don't flip on the bright lights at night. Even though you're disturbing your patients for a good reason, they resent your intruding long enough for them to become fully awake with bright lights glaring in their eyes in the middle of the night.
- Never be without a flashlight, and don't shine it right in patients' faces.
- Speak loudly enough for a patient to hear you. Speaking softly often resulted in my patient not hearing me or appreciating my subdued voice. Conversely, yelling at a

hearing-impaired patient so they could hear me did not compromise any confidential patient information provided I got them a roommate who was also hard of hearing.
- Confidentiality is a given. My early years preceded the onslaught of the education, regulation, and paperwork that surround Patient Protected Information (PPI), but we nurses understood patient privacy and common sense.
- Patients who require intensive care are not always in the intensive care unit. They can be right there on your assignment sheet when they cut loose with critically acute problems. (Hemorrhaging is one I faced more often than I cared to.) Acute problems require timely interventions, and often transferring a patient to an ICU could not happen right away. So I needed to move and treat quickly in an emergency — and no two emergencies were ever alike.

The fall semester of my second year in nursing school was the best ever! It brought obstetric (OB) nursing to life for me, and I recall that there weren't too many A's handed out by our superb instructor. Two of them were to me and another woman who had eight children and a few grandchildren. We laughed at that, as I was so ready to be a mother by that time, and she had already been there, done that, and then some. By the end of the semester, I was newly pregnant with our first child. I REALLY got a lot out of OB!

Until then, I thought I might like to be a pediatric nurse, as I love kids, but OB changed that — and so did having my own children. I wanted to make sure I would give my own children every bit of attention they needed. I was also afraid I would become overly sentimental about sick children in a hospital, and I didn't want to bring my grief over them home to my family. So in order to best serve my children, I chose to not make children a part of my nursing life. I still believe that was the right choice for me then and now.

That said, I have known several pediatric nurses over the years who were also parents, and I believe they handled their own children as caringly and capably as they did their patients. That is the beauty of nursing: we all have different likes and dislikes, strengths and weaknesses, and we can usually see what will suit us best in becoming the best we can be in our profession.

Obstetric nursing was such a high point in my nursing education that whatever followed was bound to be something of a letdown. Such was my next semester in psychiatric nursing. Whether it was the instructor constantly calling me Mom when I was not yet a mother, or just the way the program was put together, or simply a lack of comfort in the field, I knew that psychiatric nursing was not for me. So I sought to gain insight I could use in caring for any patient. I didn't earn the family-required A, but a B satisfied me just fine, and my husband and mother-in-law had the good sense not to mess with a pregnant woman. The glow of my new pregnancy had carried me through the semester. Nothing could spoil that!

My last semester in school involved more medical-surgical nursing in the team-leading section. I didn't enjoy team-leading as a hospital nurse staffing model then, and I don't today. I saw no purpose for a designated charge nurse to carry around a clipboard, following doctors in and out of rooms and taking notes about their directions for patients. To be sure, we have to know what doctors are planning, ordering, and expecting in the care of their patients. But I saw no need to follow them so closely, unless it was perhaps to remind them to wash their hands before they went into the next room. Per their orders, we wrote reams of notes on our nursing care. Why couldn't the doctors themselves write down their orders and expectations so we nurses could read them, note them, and execute them, making the care of our patients collegial? As a student, I didn't have a vote in this scenario, but did recognize it was not the nurse staffing system for me.

I wanted to know what was going on with my patients — all of it. I didn't want one nurse giving medications, one being in charge, one provider giving baths and doing vital signs, or whatever. My concern wasn't whether others would give quality care to my patients. I simply wanted to be a nurse who could provide whatever need a patient had at the time, not one who had to say she would go find the medication nurse or tell the nursing aide that the patient wanted their bath now or their bed changed. Without my experience of complete patient care at Sparrow Hospital, I might not have felt as strongly about this nurse staffing model. Years later, I do not like it any better. However, I have seen it work better in some hospitals such as Walter Reed. The military typically works as a team with varying levels of personnel responsibility, making team staffing more natural in military hospitals.

Let me clarify that I deeply respect every nursing category and player I have ever worked with in any healthcare setting. Disregard for other caregivers was never my issue with the hospital team leading model of nurse staffing. I simply did not like not having a full handle on my patients, knowing and meeting their needs, when working on a medical-surgical unit. I feared I would miss something I needed to know about a patient more than I worried about other team members not doing their job.

In certain areas of nursing care, such as home care or hospice, you realize the importance of every caregiver in your patients' homes. Where, for instance, would hospice patients be without the bath and comfort care provided by their loyal aides? And if we RNs are in a patient's home during that bath and it's easier on the patient to have two helpers, then we RNs had best lend a hand.

In many areas of nursing, the teamwork of several layers of caregivers, family, and volunteers is extremely valuable, and I love working within a team in these areas. There is no nursing function that is too menial when it comes to meeting or exceeding a patient's needs, and no player's role is unimportant. Over the years, the jobs that I sought always involved the best teamwork from all players, and I have been blessed to find many such jobs.

Chapter Three

Bringing It On — Slowly

I graduated summa cum laude, so I definitely passed, and I enjoyed proud approval at home. I had met my husband and mother-in-law's expectations. I felt that I had a great start as a beginner both at nursing and at being a mom. Although I knew I wanted to be a labor and delivery (L&D) nurse, I was perfectly willing to follow the advice of instructors and further my experience in medical-surgical nursing. I returned to the same floor where I had been a nursing extern and found that to be a good decision. Being six months pregnant when I got my associate degree in nursing, I decided to work part-time.

I was in great health, but I did not want to overdo it, and after two strenuous, nonstop years of schooling, I was ready for at least a little break. Besides, I had a baby coming — I needed to prepare! Our house needed a thorough cleaning as well, and our yard some attention.

When I took my State Boards, I was eight-plus months pregnant and great with child. I didn't worry about passing the exam; my main preoccupation was in knowing where the ladies room was and having a proctor handy enough of the time for my frequent trips. I had studied with my usual nursing friends, and we all passed with flying colors. Onward!

Floating on the cloud of anticipation of being a mom, learning my profession, and passing State Boards, I had a super summer. I worked part-time until September 1, when I decided I needed to quit working because our baby was due on the 24th.

During my last trimester, I developed an allergy and had to take Benadryl, which made me very sleepy indeed. We didn't learn until later that my in-laws' cat, Tiki, was the problem. The last month or two of my pregnancy, I moved from chair to chair at home, and he always followed me. He had come to us two years before to stay for a couple of weeks, which somehow became two years. We gave him back a couple of weeks before my due date, though, as he was not always a friendly cat. Surprise, surprise! Allergies gone.

I had requested a three-month maternity leave. I learned to never again quit work early for that reason, because our firstborn son, Clay, was about three weeks late — and yes, they let you go over your due date that much in 1972. I gained a lot more firsthand knowledge about obstetrics during that time. I learned that the cold, hard X-ray tables one had to lie on for pelvimetry Xrays were not at all comfortable, with or without a contraction. I discovered that one can go for days with contractions every five minutes, and I learned that my doctor could be far more patient than I was. I also found that there is no substitute for a good bunch of labor and delivery nurses — and I had the best. They got me through it, and our child was born.

I also found out what meconium aspiration is about, as Clay had plenty of it; but thankfully, due to prompt care in delivery, he never got sick from it. Seeing the joy on my nurses' faces and the delight of my doctor at a successful delivery reaffirmed my feeling that labor and delivery was the place for me when I returned from maternity leave. As hard as they worked helping me and the many others who were delivering around the same time, I knew that if they could be so delighted with every birth, exhausted as they had to be, I could be that happy too. It would be well worth it. Now, as then, my feelings remain the same: it was always worth it — every last one of my years in labor and delivery.

A quick word here about nurse mothers. I had not been a nurse for long when I had our first son, and I quickly realized that despite childbirth classes, newborn care classes, and nursing school, plus a B.A. in political science, I KNEW

NOTHING! Now, I'm not suggesting that all new mothers who are nurses are as clueless as I was, but I'll bet that many will agree with the principle I discovered: It's your own baby, stupid, not someone else's. My caregiving didn't run according to an eight- or twelve-hour shift. It was 24/7, day in and day out. Oh my, what a shock! When was I off duty?

I thought I knew most of what I needed to do for day-to-day care until I'd been home for a couple of days. Then Clay's cord fell off and the little stump bled a bit. Could I go to sleep? Could he go to sleep? Would he bleed to death during the two hours when he might sleep?

With great good sense, I picked up the phone and called the nursery at Sparrow Hospital. They reassured me that Clay would not exsanguinate during the night. I could sleep for whatever time was granted me before he was hungry yet again. Bliss! I rechecked his little umbilicus, then happily went to sleep for an hour or two. I am sure I called that same nursery again before Clay was out of the newborn stage. I kept wondering, though: When was my vacation?

I commend every great OB nurse who ever helped a nursing mother get the hang of nursing and who helped troubleshoot any problems. These nurses are a great comfort! In 1972, most new moms bottle-fed their infants, and nurses helped with both types of feedings. Nurses were far less likely to encourage a mother to keep breastfeeding if she showed signs that nursing was not the right thing for her, or if the baby indicated that it was not in his or her best interest.

Today, due to the proven benefits of breastfeeding, many moms use numerous tools and personnel to establish and maintain nursing. You might have one or more lactation consultants. You may get a follow-up call or visit from a hospital mother or baby nurse. You might even get a nursing consultant along with your pediatrician. There are books — lots of books. There are pumps (electric or hand) and breast shields; a wide array of nursing bras, nightgowns, and robes; and creams galore for easing sore breasts. It's amazing!

We didn't have nearly as much in 1972. We survived, though, as did our babies. Many of us even gave up breastfeeding when our babies were around six weeks old, even if we did not go back to work at that time, and we didn't feel all that guilty. Some of us just could not see the end of our babies' eating every hour or two. We had reason to think this way, and years down the road we feel immensely validated when our children, now nearing forty, continue to eat every hour or two.

The mother-child bond can be strong and healthy no matter which method of feeding is used. That's one thing I learned in my years of labor and delivery and mother/baby nursing. It's the love that makes the difference — the willingness to give and give, taking great joy in nurturing a child's life throughout the years and through all the ups and downs. That holds true for dads as well. Men cannot nurse their children, but consider the strong bonds between fathers and children whom you know. It's about nurturing, and accepting a child just for who that child is, and encouraging his or her potential.

I returned to my medical-surgical unit when I was three months postpartum, and boy was I ready! That's when the real beauty of nursing hit me: I could work part-time! Or I could work as needed — I had a choice. I chose part-time, eight-hour shifts. That way I could have adult conversations and activity part of the time yet also have my son most of the time. When I could not be home, my husband usually was, so we did not need a babysitter much in those early years. Our son had his parents the greater part of the time.

I can never recall a time when I was not happy to go to work. And I was even happier to return home to my family. What I gained from my time away was priceless in helping me to know myself and be a better wife and mother. I put that time to good use by honing my nursing skills, paying attention to on-the-spot learning, and enjoying the camaraderie of the staff on my unit. I also filled in and helped when I could without taking too much time away from home and family.

Working part-time evenings, I would call home and check in with my husband to make sure our son was okay. Did he eat well? Cry much? Have any problems? Jim always answered nonchalantly. Everything was fine, he told me. He seemed to wonder why I asked so many needless questions. One night he mentioned that he couldn't find our son's pacifier when he put him to bed, and I was immediately alarmed that he would have a fight on his hands to get Clay to sleep. Not so — no problem. When I came home from work, I found and promptly disposed of the pacifier. That's how our kids gave up their pacifiers: Dad couldn't find them, the children went to sleep, and every pacifier in the house magically disappeared. I must have thought that I should have the big solution for the ominous task of discontinuing a pacifier. After all, I was a nurse. Hah! Common sense, as in most things, wins the day.

Eventually I sought to move to labor and

delivery, my dream in nursing care. A wise department head in maternal child nursing determined that I could do so, but I would need to start in postpartum, taking care of moms and also newborns when they were with their moms. In the early 1970s, "rooming in" was not around. The babies came out to the moms for feedings, and then the babies went back to the nurseries. Moms could rest. Moms could take sitz baths.

Those who had a cesarean section stayed for about a week. Vaginal delivery moms required three to four days. That is not the way it is today, but back then we solved some problems before they mushroomed, we gave great care, and we had the time to follow through. I believe moms and dads went home with their newborns feeling like they knew a little bit. This was before insurance companies began to tell the medical profession just how much time was acceptable (translation: payable) for a new mom and baby to stay in the hospital. Now the government is telling us what is acceptable. Many of us in healthcare are not happy with this direction.

I went to postpartum on the evening shift, and worked under a charge nurse who must have invented postpartum. She certainly had the routine down pat! I was cautioned, prodded, and reviewed on passing out Senokot (a laxative) to moms promptly at 8 o'clock in the evening. I didn't then, and I don't now, know why this designated time was written in stone for efficacy of said laxative, but by golly, that's when we were supposed to deliver it to all patients. God forbid we should be called down to the recovery room to assist moms who had just delivered — the Senokot might be delayed! Never mind that the recovery room was overflowing and we needed to get patients recovered, stable, and transferred up to postpartum so they could rest and get to see their newborns, who were already in the nursery.

I enjoyed helping new moms — heck, I still was a new mom myself! However, the urgency of some of the routines escaped me. What I found satisfying were the opportunities to teach one-on-one, handle any problems, and help moms in whatever ways they needed. This job gave me the greatest clue as to what I liked best in nursing care: dealing with the unexpected and non-routine. The occasional emergency or acute problem on postpartum did not fall into the normal patterns of my unit. They left plenty of room for good nursing judgment, as most acute problems are best caught at the very early stages.

But if labor and delivery was drowning with patients and needed help from my department, I volunteered. That was where I wanted to be. And I never had much competition — my fellow postpartum nurses were glad to let me volunteer.

Another delivery was coming my way: number two child! I was due on August 1st of 1974, and that is when I had our second son, Brian — a perfectly handsome, healthy-appearing, beautiful little man. He resembled my father, whom I adored.

I had a great pregnancy and worked right up to my due date, which was far better for my mental health. I had learned from my first pregnancy not to just sit around that last month. Among other things, Brian's birth taught me that I could work right up to my due date and still have enough energy for labor.

I also learned that sometimes a child can look perfect on the outside but be imperfect on the inside. Brian started turning blue when he was a day-and-a-half old and starting to get livelier. An X-ray revealed an enlarged heart, and our son was immediately placed on oxygen and transferred to a local hospital that specialized in cardiovascular needs. I was discharged, too, with my donut ring for sitting comfort, and my husband and I followed Brian's ambulance an hour or two later.

Cardiac catheterization revealed that our son had a condition which, at that time, was a grave threat to life. He had ventricular hypertrophy and a tiny mitral valve; oxygenated blood was not flowing well through his system. Brian's heart had stopped during this catheterization, but the team was able to revive him and planned to replace the mitral valve with one that could function more effectively so his vital organs could receive the life-giving oxygen they needed. It was the only solution available at the time, the doctors explained, and it was temporary. Brian would need repeated procedures as he grew and would have to live a more sedentary life due to his compromised cardiac function.

But our son arrested yet again before the valve that was flown in could be inserted. A backup valve was also being flown in so the surgeons could provide the best match. But it was not to be. I always hoped that those valves eventually helped some other child.

Bad things happen to everyone, nurses and their families included. Brian had excellent, compassionate care. All that could be done for him was done, and I could even feel somewhat comfortable going home that first night to sleep, as a friend of mine from nursing school was taking care of him. If he could be touched, picked up, and loved, she would do it. My husband and I could go home for a while to sleep and pray, knowing he was in good hands. Compassionate and great caregivers will give you every chance to do what you can for your critically ill baby. They will call him by his name, and they will comfort you when he dies.

We can't save everybody; some conditions are just not compatible with life. But I learned that I could pour a whole lot of love into four days of life with my child, added onto the nine months of loving anticipation. And I learned that I could move forward after his loss, cherishing and loving those whom God has left in my care.

Many are not as lucky as I. They can never have children, nor do they already have a child as happy and healthy as the one we had at home. I discovered how my loving husband and our twenty-two-month-old son — along with my parents, family members and friends, and my strong belief in God's plan for my family — could sustain me through my grief and give me hope for the future. A loss such as ours can offer perspective and a willingness to help others who grieve.

I returned to work part-time six weeks later. But first I met with the head of the maternal child department, who had offered me my position in postpartum a year earlier. I told her I was ready to go to labor and delivery. She agreed and asked me if I would like to work eight-hour nights, four nights on and ten off, to relieve one of the full-time night nurses. I accepted, and I simply loved it! I trained with the best. In those early days back in 1974, the older women who cared for the labor patients struck me as so motherly, even grandmotherly. They had such a special gift. I wanted to grow up to be just like them!

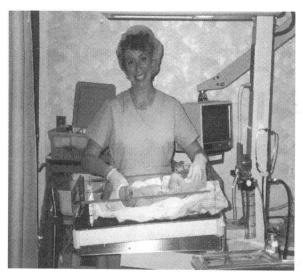

I learned to stock equipment and supplies in the labor and delivery areas so they would always be available when I needed them. I learned a whole lot about anticipatory nursing, which has always been helpful.

Most deliveries were happy with great outcomes, but some were not. The pit of your stomach can drop out when you're assessing a new patient for fetal heart tones and find none. You have to comfort the mom and family any way you can as they undergo ultrasound to determine whether they have a live child inside.

In crisis situations, a team of providers and family members might decide what could or should be done to save a child. In the years before neonatal intensive care units were common, small special-care nurseries were sometimes available, where doctors, nurses, and families could convene and decide what interventions to do for a very ill newborn. That was nursing care at its best; we nurses were partners in health-care decisions — even the most difficult ones.

I seldom came to work part-time, or even full-time, without being asked by the head nurse to work an extra shift — or two, or three — to make up for short staffing. I have never known a hospital to be overstaffed. I said yes often, knowing how it felt to work with fewer nurses than the patient acuity required. I also knew that many whom I worked with did not have as flexible a working situation as I did, with great help at home. During most of my early nursing years, my husband took over what home duties he could, never complaining that he had too many childcare hours in addition to his busy work schedule, which was full-time and then some.

Working in labor and delivery led me to some eye-opening discoveries. I learned, for instance, that an older lady who had never married nor been a mother could make a first-class labor and delivery nurse. And an irascible, opinionated, but clinically excellent nurse could be exactly what our labor patients needed. For sure, I found out how fast labor and delivery emergencies can happen — in the blink of an eye, and sometimes at the same time as other emergencies. We never turned away a pregnant patient, no matter how busy we were or whether we had a room available. All stayed and we coped.

Having 300 to 400 deliveries a month could work out pretty evenly — or not. We might have twenty deliveries one day and one or two the next. The number of deliveries, of course, says nothing about all the care hours our patients in labor and delivery received before they were discharged or transferred to another unit. Flexibility and multi-tasking took on a whole new meaning for me. Documentation was another nightmare; it created many hours of charting after the next shift came on and we were relieved of patient care duties. Even then, an occasional emergency sometimes preempted charting, delaying it still further. When we couldn't get to the patient chart, we used pillow cases, monitoring strips, paper towels, even our scrubs, to jot down the time we completed a task or made an observation. Somehow the ink all came off in the hospital laundry.

We often completed admissions after deliveries in a sort of two-for-one, processing both mom and baby or at least handling the formalities of the admissions process. We had already asked all the questions and made the needed observations for admission while doing whatever else needed to be done. Recording them on paper was another matter. We knew that if it was not charted, it was not done, as any good malpractice attorney will tell you; however, the irreversible timelines for most of our patient care needs did not often lend themselves to orderly charting. So we coped, again and again, and we had good outcomes.

In that kind of nursing, nurses hope to build a trusting relationship with the attending doctors, as we are there for the whole labor and delivery process while the doctors generally are not. Sometimes they're not available when you really need them, or they may come flying in on a wing and a prayer. We often wondered whether doctors could somehow know that a patient was going to crash and get back to labor and delivery in time for that crash. But it didn't usually happen that way — or if a doc did have a notion that something might go awry, he could be knee-deep in patient care or in a surgery. (Or on the golf course for some much-needed recreation. Ssssshhh!)

We learned that we were all human — no exceptions. We could and did make mistakes and errors in judgment. Regardless, great teamwork and mutual professional respect got the work at hand done, and done well. Occasionally an OB doctor would whine about being called in too early — the patient wasn't right on the brink of delivery or took a little longer than expected. That happens. Labor and delivery is not a perfect science; gut feeling is a whole lot of it, as well as experience. We did not tolerate a lot of that kind of criticism.

I knew I had earned the doctors' trust when the OB medical director began calling me the "old lady" at the tender age of twenty-seven. I felt like I had gotten to the top of the mountain. But I also knew that staying there would take continued excellent work with our patients. That was fine — it was already my goal.

Boy, did we have a lot of doctors! That's because we were a teaching hospital, with not one but two medical schools at Michigan State University down the road just ten minutes. We had MD and DO students and residents. Nursing students, too, from the Registered Nursing programs at MSU and Lansing Community

College, both of which vied for spots in hospitals. There was an LPN program at LCC too, but we did not have LPN students in labor and delivery. A few LPNs scrubbed for our cesarean sections and other surgical procedures, but they had already been surgical scrub nurses when they came to us and needed minimal training. At that time, LPNs did not do labor nursing care.

Nurses, residents, and medical students had varying responses to working in labor and delivery. Dedicated labor and delivery nurses are very passionate about working in this specialty, recognizing that many nurses do not share the same passion — ever! The practice of pulling nurses from other units to work in labor and delivery seldom works. Many labor and delivery units are "closed units" whose nursing staff members guarantee that they will cover their own staffing needs. Registered Nursing students and medical students, however, are required to do a semester rotation in labor and delivery; it is not optional.

When resident doctors came our way, we knew that their programs required it. That was fine when it involved OB residents — it was almost always good to have their help. They wanted to be there, learn the ropes, and get to the big leagues as full-fledged obstetrician-gynecologists. Family practice or emergency room residents were another matter. I have never met an emergency room team member, whether a doctor or otherwise, who wanted to do deliveries or manage pregnancy or labor issues. No one got swept through the ER faster than a woman with a suspiciously round belly; such patients were immediately levitated up to labor and delivery. Sometimes they came so fast that the transport person who brought them practically bolted before the patient in the wheelchair was even up to the L&D nursing station!

A few years later, when I had the opportunity to see plenty of ER as a house supervisor, I watched the ER team eagerly and efficiently handle everything from a totally crushed body to an impalement victim with a pole through the chest. But a labor patient? Noooooooooo — whisked from the ER before she even knew she had passed through it. A man could just as easily have been sent our way if he had a Santa belly! Those contractions... the ER folks just did not want to deal with them, and certainly not with a birthing.

Family practice residents generally seemed okay with their L&D rotation, but a lot of them went right out into practice and decided to ditch being an L&D provider. This was often because of time constraints due to their overcrowded offices. But as time passed, it also became more of a medical-legal decision, because the cost of doing business went up exponentially in legal overhead with L&D-provider status.

That was a fact I grew to hate. As the litigious climate that affected obstetric cases grew, with ambulance chasers lurking in every corner, excellent doctors who liked the whole realm of family care left OB in droves. And family practice doctors weren't the only ones; sometimes an OB-GYN decided to limit his or her practice to gynecology due to the skyrocketing number of junk lawsuits. I saw way too many great doctors leave OB. When I asked one of my favorites, whom I called Dr. P., why he was giving up the obstetrics part of his practice, he shook his head and said quietly, "Syl, it's just not fun anymore." His response made me want to just sit down and cry.

We continued to take care of our patients with our other doctors. Some of those docs we might have been willing to part with. The patients had their favorites and so did we — that's just human nature. The worst side of that nature, though, has been patients and lawyers who willingly destroy a professional practice and reputation for monetary rewards based on no credible fault of the professional. Credible, provable injury of course deserves compensation; baseless charges do not.

Starting work in labor and delivery after losing my own newborn was difficult at times. But I found that I could give laboring and new moms the best nursing care possible to achieve positive outcomes for mom and baby. I wanted to deliver the compassionate care mothers need when they're going through the challenge of a new birth. And I wanted every single patient to experience the special joy that only a newborn can bring: new life and hope for a future with that child, whether it's a mother's first or fifth. Were there sometimes problems and sad outcomes with all those births over the years? Of course. But you learn how to give the help that is needed with those as well.

My third pregnancy was a long nine months. I worked lots of hours in L&D with numerous high-risk labor patients. That was therapeutic, for I realized I was not alone in having the joy of a newborn turn into loss and unbelievable sorrow. My husband and I looked forward to having our third child not as a replacement for our lost son, but because we were anticipating a new life, with all the uniqueness that child would bring. We looked forward with joy to the arrival, and we have never been disappointed; our Beth has been a light in our lives in her own special way, right from the start. God took back one, but he has given us our Clay and Beth now for forty and thirty-seven years, respectively. We are blessed by and thankful for our two wonderful children.

Although family is always first with me, I have found that there is enough love in me both for my loved ones and for giving to others in the special ways good nursing care can offer. After my three-month maternity leave for Beth, I returned part-time to L&D in 1976, ready to continue the work that I loved. I decided to work evenings again, and that proved ideal. I could spend the better part of the day with our children, then hire a high school sitter for a couple of hours until my husband got home. He took over the feedings, meals, bathing, bedtime routines, and so forth, so that and when I arrived home, I could relax, put up my feet, and enjoy some quiet time before going to bed.

That quiet time just by myself to unwind was necessary. I could have a snack, read a good book, or just sit in an easy chair and stare at the wall. I was young and could deal with little sleep. That came with the territory of having little ones who awakened at the crack of dawn or during the night, when I would comfort them till they fell back asleep. Most of the nurses I worked with on the evening shift were in the same situation, so we often got together with our children for lunch or late morning and let the kids play together while we visited — then went to work later.

We had a great team, and we got the work done that needed to be done, whether we left at 11:30 or in the wee hours of the morning. We left knowing there was enough help to do the care needed. Laboring women have an uncanny knack of delivering or having emergencies during shift changes, which creates problems for timely changeover. Besides, when we had worked with one or more patients for hours and they wound up delivering at change of shift, we kind of liked to stay and finish the deal. We had a lot of skin in the game by that time, so sticking around was never a chore. And the patients were so very grateful that the extra time simply melted away.

Here again, having great support at home was huge. The only thing my husband ever asked of me was to have the security guards walk me out to my car if it was night and I was alone. I tried to comply, I really did. But there were a couple of times when, in my tired fog, I trotted out to my car in the dark, with no humans in sight. The guards were wise to us, though. They would hang out by the emergency door where we nurses usually exited and escort us to our vehicles.

For many years, I had a persistent bruise on one hip. It was inflicted by the sharp corner of a table, which managed to always catch me as I raced to a delivery room with a patient on a cart. I tried hard to get my patients to the delivery rooms with a little time to spare, but that didn't always work, and emergencies could send me hustling. In 1976, deliveries were accomplished in delivery rooms, not labor rooms, unless a little one came very precipitously. Sudden deliveries happened, usually without a doctor present. With so many residents, students, and doctors around, why did some women deliver attended only by a nurse? It just happens! Residents have meetings, rounds, surgeries, more rounds, problem-solving on the floors, and so on. Some babies just don't wait, and some moms don't have any warning that the baby is coming now. Then suddenly, voila — there's the baby! So we nurses learn that we can deliver an infant in a pinch, though we much prefer that the doctor do it.

One of my more memorable labor and delivery experiences involved a very nice, healthy young woman whose husband was a large-animal veterinarian. As she progressed through her labor, her husband kept recommending birthing practices, offering advice that was more pertinent to a cow than a woman. His wife — the one who was actually having the baby — finally had enough and asked him to leave the room if he would not quit with his suggestions for herself and the staff caring for her.

The woman finally wound up with a cesarean section for failure to progress in labor. Her system just wouldn't cooperate by producing effective contractions. Fortunately, this was before fathers were allowed in delivery rooms and C-sections; otherwise, we probably would have been lectured on how to pull a calf!

These early years in L&D were also before the existence of full-fledged neonatal intensive care units with designated staff to attend high-risk, premature deliveries. The movement toward such units was gaining ground, though. Often we had only the delivery RN to attend the mom and baby, and that could get interesting when both had immediate needs at the same time. We managed, though, with our OB doctors and each other, putting on the emergency light when there were critical needs. I cannot say enough of the great teamwork we had — doctors, nurses, housekeepers, aides, ward secretaries, house supervisors, and others. When we nurses in labor and delivery hollered, someone came, even an occasional stray doctor.

Our special care nursery opened on the same floor as labor and delivery, right around the corner, and before long, babies were just about hanging off the walls in this little room. There was such a need for specialized newborn care for ill and premature babies! We helped out there as we could, though not often, as our needs for labor and delivery care were too great. We were, however, awesome at transporting ill newborns over there swiftly after jump-starting them in delivery.

My early years in L&D were before the onslaught of numerous scheduled procedures such as scheduled labor inductions and cesarean sections. However, we did do some such procedures. We did our own tubal ligations; the patients just had to come down to us from the postpartum floor. Lacking designated OB anesthesia personnel at the time, we had to rely on the surgery unit to send us an anesthesiologist for emergency C-sections or scheduled C-sections and tubal ligations. Almost to a man or woman, the surgery anesthesia personnel heartily disliked coming to labor and delivery. They hated dealing with the unknown, not knowing the patient before they put them to sleep, especially in emergencies. We tried to do things their way, setting up IV tubing the way they liked it, providing all the necessities plus extras in the rooms, still the anesthesiologists complained.

We could not do our surgeries without them, so we coped.

We did have a couple of nurse anesthetists at this time, but they were not allowed to put people to sleep for surgeries. They were restricted to helping with resuscitation needs for newborns, handling some local anesthesia, administering nitrous gas, and assisting anesthesiologists with intubation. It was several years before the nurse anesthetists could do epidurals, spinals, cesarean sections, and other general anesthesia procedures under the supervision of an OB anesthesiologist. When we moved to the new unit and got our own OB anesthesiologist, dedicated only to our L&D unit, we thought we had died and gone to heaven! The OB anesthesiologists worked well with the nurse anesthetists, and L&D could now take care of its own anesthesia needs. This has been a very good thing, with an epidural rate as high as 90 percent or greater at times in the last twenty or more years, and no fewer emergency needs.

In the mid to late 1970s, we did things a bit differently than common L&D practices today. Not everyone had an IV. We did mini-shaves in the area that counted and gave admission enemas and sometimes an admission shower. Fetal monitors were available, but most did not have to be on all the time unless the patient was high-risk. Women did not have birth plans; they took what we offered and didn't ask many questions. Every last woman said, "I can't!" when we asked them to slide from their labor bed to a stretcher to go to delivery. But they managed when they realized the end was in sight. Eventually we got around to having fathers in delivery, but they were usually excluded if we anticipated problems.

We created preference cards for all the delivering doctors, and we followed them item-by-item so the doctors could have the supplies they wanted or might need. Then life was good! We learned that Pitocin could be given in various ways after or even during childbirth to help the uterus contract and to minimize bleeding. Woe to the nurse who gave it at a time or in a way that the delivering doctor did not want it given! Some docs were quite precise (isn't that a nice word!) in their preferences, and accommodating their preferences as best we could helped maintain collegial working relationships.

No labor and delivery nursing experience would be complete without having a patient wheeled up to L&D hollering, "The baby is coming!" as the poor ER transport tech raced with the stretcher or wheelchair! The tech was always directed right back to the delivery area, and a nurse followed to help whisk the patient over to the delivery table and see what was happening, flipping on the infant warmer as she raced by. Sometimes the woman was right: the baby was coming and we had a delivery — no muss, no fuss. But occasionally the woman was not even pregnant. Red-faced, huffing and puffing, we then wondered, what now? Did we need to admit someone not even pregnant?

Those were not easy questions to answer. And as you might guess, such incidents never happened when the unit was slow, so we had to leave behind other patients briefly or with fewer nurses to assist them while we dealt with these odd situations. I often wondered whether anything I had learned during my semester in psych nursing might help here. Nothing popped into my mind, though, so I just winged it. And yes, the kind of situation I've described happened more than once in my L&D years. Assisting with a precipitous delivery, even on the elevator or in ER, was much easier to handle; it was far lower on the weird scale.

By and large we had great relationships with the doctors. They learned they could trust us, and we learned we could trust them. When we called for orders, most of them would say to us, "What do they need?" The doctors almost always went along with our requests. They gave verbal orders and followed up as needed; they recognized that we helped them manage their patients, and they were grateful. Often a nurse would find herself dealing one-on-one with more than one patient at the same time. A doctor would then step in and help, or perhaps another nurse who was freer at that time.

One of our OB-GYNs relaxed in the kitchen one evening, eating the food we had brought in that night for potluck. He remarked that, L&D nursing skills aside, we sure could cook. He was right — we were good cooks! We ate anything anyone brought in, because meals were not frequently enjoyed at the traditional time or any set time in a shift. We were grateful for any contributions the doctors might bring, too. We even choked down some near-rotten bananas one of our OB residents brought in once for banana splits. Nothing could taste too bad with all that ice cream, chocolate, and other goodies piled on top!

When our doctors came in for deliveries, they often had to wait a bit, so they had time to tell stories. We learned that when one of our favorite docs said "purple smoke" to his wife over the phone, it didn't mean he was smoking some questionable substance; it meant that he was on his way home. This OB-GYN had been a flight surgeon during World War II, and "purple smoke" referred to the flights returning home to base.

Another of our OB-GYNs told us that if we didn't make time to go to the bathroom during our prolonged shifts, he was going to line us all up and do bladder repairs when we hit forty years of age. (He didn't, of course, offer to help us with our patients so we could take those potty breaks.) And a resident doctor learned that the way to get help from a pregnant nurse wasn't to say, "Wow, Sylvia, you sure are looking great with child! Can you come help me with this patient?" (Sure, I helped — the patient. The doctor may have had to fend for himself.)

Our work in L&D could be a physical challenge. In a silly conversation one night, we counted the ways:

- Never sitting down for an eight- or twelve-hour shift or even a double shift
- Getting bitten
- Getting kicked
- Doing some nursing care maneuvers upside-down or in otherwise compromising positions
- Applying enough fundal pressure to help the baby get out
- Bending over for hours on end doing various tasks such as helping moms push

out their babies
- Helping to clean up all the messiness — and boy, could our patients make messes!
- Never having a chance to eat
- Never having a chance to visit the restroom
- Never getting more than a sip of coffee!
- Holding up a unit of blood or IV fluids and squeezing them so they would go in faster — for a long time
- Mopping up delivery rooms or labor rooms when our poor aides were overwhelmed and we needed a room right away
- Transporting patients on stretchers from labor and delivery rooms, to the recovery room, then up one floor to postpartum — fast, if it was an emergency run
- Running up and down to the lab, either to get units of blood to administer to a patient or to take blood samples down to the lab for testing
- Going down to ER to get pregnant or laboring patients with wheelchairs or stretchers
- Encouraging patients to stay on the delivery table when they suddenly decided they did not wish to deliver (safety measures, y'all!)

There were more such physical demands, but

you get the idea. It was work — real work! And to complicate matters, occasionally a woman did not want to be there having a baby. It might be an unplanned pregnancy, or the woman was fighting with the baby's father or significant other, or she would rather have been at home delivering. Different cultures have different birthing practices, and we learned a lot about them. We did our best to deliver the care needed the way our patients desired, but sometimes that just wasn't possible, fetal or maternal risks being the determining factors.

Women in pre-term labor did not like the solutions for stopping labor that were current standards of care. For example, when I first started in L&D, the treatment of choice for pre-term labor was an alcohol IV drip — slowly, of course. Women just did not appreciate the ill effects they suffered with these treatments, which were much like what someone drinking too much alcohol might suffer.

Other solutions weren't much better. Women could experience excessive flushing, heart racing, anxiety, nausea, sleepiness, blood pressure changes, and so forth. They grew tired of having blood drawn for the repeated lab testing that ensured their safety during certain treatments. Women didn't want to be confined to hospital bed rest, either, yet they were often kept for days or even weeks.

In response to the needs of the growing high-risk pregnancy population, antepartum units arose. These were designed to care for women who had not yet delivered but who needed certain procedures regularly, or who were on bed rest and/or medications for pre-term labor, or who had other needs which the OB doctor felt needed skilled nursing observation and doctor/facility resources. Some moms ended up in this type of unit after a birth, too, if they continued to present serious risk factors that required care management not easily provided on a regular postpartum floor.

I was often in charge of evening shifts, taking my turn along with the rest. There wasn't a whole lot of difference between my nurse friends and me; we all cared for patients and helped each other. Yet much to my surprise, one of the weekend house supervisors asked me if I would like to do relief supervision on the day shift every other weekend, opposite her weekends.

My first thought was, heck no! I wanted to work the weekends when she worked, as she was a great supervisor, always willing to provide help when we needed it. My second thought was amazement that she would ask me to consider house supervision. I was twenty-nine years old and had worked only on a surgical unit and in labor and delivery. What did I know of the whole hospital?

But the supervisor persisted at trying to recruit me, so I gave the matter some thought. I could continue to help L&D now and then during the week and work the eight-hour weekend days when my husband was home. I would be able to meet more of our kids' needs during the week and need little outside childcare. So finally I said yes, provisionally, and requested to train with this supervisor.

I was almost horrified that I had agreed to do the job. The responsibility of having to know what was happening in an entire 500-bed hospital weighed on me. I knew little about many of the nursing units and the people who worked in them. My supervisor friend said, "No problem. Much of it is just common sense, and you have that." She also reassured me that I would always have a backup suit-and-tie administrator. At first I didn't find that as comforting as knowing that I could call my friend if I got stuck, but I came to know better. The administrators were helpful every time I needed them.

The day came when I was riding in an elevator and one of the orthopedic surgeons saw my name tag, chuckled, and said I was too young to be a supervisor — and I was able to actually smile back calmly. "I know!" I said.

Oh, what experiences this new job brought! My supervisor friend was right about its taking mostly common sense, but it took me awhile to see what that involved. It was mostly about making logical decisions.

There were some staff members whom I could rely on every time to fill staffing needs during a crisis. However, I went after the ones who were less inclined to help out in a pinch, and a better sense of teamwork often resulted. The discoveries continued in other ways as well. For instance, I learned that...

- with administrative approval, unplanned weekend events such as a séance can help soothe those who had suffered a tragic loss.
- one solution does not fit all, but if I was in there trying for all, my efforts were usually noticed and valued.
- learning the names of the workers on all the units I dealt with every weekend had great value. It meant a lot to the staff that I learned to pronounce and spell their names correctly.
- I could answer a call light while walking down the hall on any unit and help in some way, even if it was just to provide the reassurance of a prompt response.

- a 500-bed hospital has a lot of activity going on in it. Having spent a few years in the contained and hectic world of laboring and postpartum women, I found a whole new hospital world opening up for me. I found that I could scrub in for an emergency cesarean section while on duty as house supervisor. It was all a matter of meeting the most critical need of the moment and having the experience to do so. It's amazing what can go on in a hospital!

Probably the most valuable management skill I acquired was the ability to determine what information I needed in order to meet the patient care and staffing needs of each unit. I had neither the time nor interest for gossip — it didn't help me ensure that the nurses could do their jobs efficiently and effectively. What I, and all of us nurses, needed to know was, what did our patients need in order to ensure their best outcomes? I didn't care who was getting a divorce, who was sleeping with whom, who had gained too much weight, or who didn't want to work with another coworker. What interested me was whether a unit had the right equipment and staff, or whether correct protocols were being followed for high-risk situations, or what steps could be taken to resolve a problem. I didn't always have an answer, but I learned that it was okay to say that I didn't but would find out as soon as possible. It was about using my resources, as no one can know everything. It was about following through and establishing trust.

A house supervisor spends a fair amount of time in code situations for those whose heart has stopped, or who have quit breathing or gone into shock. I saw a lot of the emergency room and the units that were most likely to have emergencies, and I had a lot of patients flow through. Sometimes the needs were simple. I might hold a small child who had been bitten by a dog while the doctor assessed and treated the wound; or soothe a patient who was undone by a large loss of blood; or calm the parents of a suffering child while explaining what was needed to help the child; or sit with a suicide risk who had been brought in by anxious family members.

House supervisors learn to help where needed and hopefully minimize any problems before they get out of hand. Some of us also realized that spending most of our time trying to staff the current and next shifts appropriately was not how we wanted to spend the rest of our nursing lives. House supervision isn't for everyone; however, the position gave me a great standpoint to determine where I wanted to work next. I knew that I needed to get back to a role that focused more on patient care; that is just me. And my biggest desire was to work in a well-run unit with great management; those qualities are so important for meeting the needs of both patients and staff. Thus, after two years of nursing supervision, I chose to work in surgery three days a week.

The head nurse on the surgery unit was an RN of many years who also had military background. I figured the department would run with precision, with everyone knowing their role, and I was right. Surgery ran like clockwork! And this department had some real advantages besides being efficiently managed. There weren't as many pleas to cover other shifts as I was used to — hurrah! Many of the nurses had worked in surgery for years and would do so for many more, something that the surgeons in the various specialty areas found very reassuring. There were always regulars on duty for them during a normal week's surgery schedule, so they knew that even with newbies added to their cases, they would have at least some expert help.

I was reassured by the excellent surgical nurses who mentored me. But it took a while for me to earn the trust and respect of some of the surgeons. Other than the OB-GYN surgeons, who were glad if surprised to see me there, none of the surgeons looked at me as an expert — which, for sure, I was not.

My rudest awakening was a plastic surgeon who felt sure I would somehow fumble his cases and not treat them as delicately as his procedures required. I believe he thought that in doing pre-surgical scrubs, I would just slosh around the scrub rather than do it precisely. In his mind, my several years as an L&D nurse evidently translated into the conviction that I would be too careless for his cases.

But our head nurse didn't see it that way. She insisted that all the surgical nurses have a versatile capability between all the specialties. So I drew this surgeon more often than I cared for in the early times of my two years working in surgery. I decided that I would be so courteous, humble, and obedient that he would not have the rudeness to scold or badger me. I was ladylike to the extreme. I was delicate. I repeatedly asked him exactly how he would like me to do any given task so he could pontificate on his desires.

By the time I left surgery, my former critic thought I was the next best thing to sliced bread, and why on earth would I want to leave? The key was to kill him with kindness. But in turn, when he began to treat me like a fellow human, he discovered that we shared a love for horses. Win-win!

The surgeons were not the only ones who had their favorites; we nurses and operating room techs did too. My preferred areas were usually the general surgery cases or orthopedics. I even learned how to scrub in on some of these cases, although previously my only related scrubbing experience had been in cesarean sections, tubal ligations, or the rare hysterectomy that got performed in labor and delivery. Most of this learning was of the "see one, do one, teach one" variety. The principles involved — scrubbing technique, handing over instruments, keeping a surgical field sterile, and so forth — applied to most any case. But the instruments used for different procedures were sometimes very different.

For some reason, I got along well with a couple of the neurosurgeons who worked together. This surprised me, as they were demanding and specific about their helpers and wanted the experienced nurses around. I surely didn't have a great deal of experience in any kind of neurosurgery!

Learning the tools of their trade was fascinating. Between great mentors and good luck, when these two asked for something, somehow I managed to provide it. I figured that luck and prayer had a lot to do with my success. And their cases were comical, because these surgeons often acted like two kids in a playpen. Maybe that was the basis of my success! I had two kids of my own whom I sometimes had to keep the peace between. Who knew that my parenting skills could be an asset in dealing with fractious neurosurgeons!

I also liked the X-ray procedure room or any local anesthetic case. Then I had a patient who wasn't asleep, one I could actually manage and enjoy the instant gratification of knowing when my help was well-received. I asked to be in these kinds of cases often, and since I worked on the three days when they were most likely to be scheduled, I was usually granted my wish. As a result, I discovered the reason why I would willingly leave surgery when asked to do another job. It was not that I disliked either surgeons or anesthesiologists, but I tired of the conflict that often erupted between these two players. Surgeons knew they had to wait for anesthesia in order to start their cases and could not proceed without the anesthesiologist's help. They hated that — no control over that piece. It reminded me once again of the two kids in a playpen.

Furthermore, I realized that I liked much more patient contact than what I usually got in surgery. That usually was limited to verifying the patients' names and the procedures they were having, assisting them onto the surgical table, and maybe doing a prep or some such before they went to sleep or were taken over by the anesthesiologist. Even if a spinal anesthetic was given, the patient usually had enough other medication by anesthesia to be asleep throughout the procedure.

My two years in surgery came to an end when one of my favorite OB-GYN doctors asked me to manage his office. After a great deal of thought, I accepted. Once again I was to do a job I had not sought but was asked to do. It was the second such job. I'm not sure I realized at that time that I was a sucker for someone asking me to do something, but I came to understand it was part of my nature. I think it belongs to my servant mentality, a trait shared by many, even most, nurses. Nor is it known only to nursing; many professionals such as teachers, pastors, and social workers have it.

It was not easy to say yes, however, even though I loved the four doctors in this office and had a good working relationship with them all. This would be my first full-time job, and I needed to think about leaving my children five days a week regularly.

Our youngest, our daughter, was starting school, but that did not make my decision any easier. Working part-time, I had time both weekdays and weekends to enjoy being with my children. I wasn't sure I wanted to tie up all five weekdays. Would I be able to meet my family's needs or even schedule important appointments? I discussed my concerns with the doctors, and great people that they were, they acknowledged my needs as a young parent and assured me that they would accommodate my needs regarding my family.

So I accepted, and have never been sorry that I did. And the doctors kept their word to me — they flexed with my needs as a mother and wife. It was a wonderful job for four years with the four superbly professional and helpful doctors who continually worked well with all the staff.

Chapter Four

Office Work 101

What did I know about working in an office? All my experience had been in a hospital setting!

We had a small staff at this OB-GYN office but the other employees had been there awhile, and they capably eased me into the office needs and roles. It took me awhile to figure out what their idea of an office manager was. It took all of us awhile, as the doctors had not really figured it out either.

I was not trained in the business aspects of a medical practice, but I was learning day by day where improvements could be made. Since I was used to managing other staff, and since this staff was capable and hard-working, the supervision part was easy. My position was the first of several jobs in which I created and developed a new role in an existing operation.

Besides taking care of our patients, I expanded into some different roles in this office, education being a big one. I conducted classes for parents on labor and delivery, newborn care, what to expect through and after pregnancy, and the like. Sometimes I made rounds with the doctors, although another nurse had already been doing so for years. I also scrubbed with them in scheduled and sometimes emergency cesarean sections and their other gynecological surgeries. I enjoyed helping to develop all that our in-office services could offer to our OB and GYN patients.

The doctors eventually wanted me to train to do their ultrasounds, as they were getting their own machine and wanted some assistance with the more routine procedures. That request really put me in a tailspin. I was horrified to think that I would be responsible for doing credible ultrasounds, as I am not a mechanically talented person. I've often thought that people like me marry engineers because we can't fix or do much with machines of any sort ourselves. The machines I had been using in my nursing practice so far were familiar to me as I used them over and over on every shift. But ultrasound was a whole different proposal.

I was going to agree anyway, despite my concerns, when I thought of one of the LPNs in the office. She was good at mechanical things and was always the one who fixed anything at all for us. The doctors agreed to train her, and this skilled LPN was on her way to training in a jiffy. She was delighted; it meant an increase in pay for her, and she loved doing the ultrasounds. We all were pleased. She did ultrasounds for lots of years, and the last I knew, she was still doing them. Even now, when I use a recipe she shared with me many years ago, (yum!), I smile when I think of her. That was the beginning of my helping other nurses develop and fill roles that maximized their talents and desires, something I have always felt was important for ensuring excellence in nursing.

People often seem curious about nurses' working relationships with doctors. At least, the people in my life have often asked how relationships go in an office setting, where nurses work so closely with the doctors, as opposed to hospital work. An office is quite different from an area like labor and delivery, where nurses see little of the doctors until the delivery.

When you work with the best in any setting, there is good reason to believe that working relationships will be collegial. I have found this to be true. The senior partner who hired me (after approval from the other three, of course) was always a favorite of mine, bless his often grumpy little self! He became a great friend during my time at the office and remained one after I left. He was nearing retirement age and often discussed whether he should retire. I told him I thought that when the time for him to retire arrived, he would know it. Until then, why not limit his practice to what he felt like doing if he enjoyed it? His wife, whom I also got to know well, often said he should just keep working. So that is what he did.

This experienced doctor was super with patients, who never seemed to mind that he either called them "Dear" or "Tinker Bell." On any given day I could be either — though if I was in his face about cutting down on his cigarettes or the grease he ate, I was probably just a nuisance. If a female patient was having difficulties, he usually wrote a little note at the top of her record: "pms." It didn't mean pre-menstrual syndrome — it meant "poor , miserable soul." These ladies got the best of treatment; he may have even learned their names.

The other doctors were special to me as well. One of them even became my doctor. (We had a previous history: during my L&D years, I had the privilege of helping him and his wife give birth to their youngest child.) All of them treated me as a professional, and working relationships were always collegial and supportive. Before I left the practice, we even got a fifth doctor — a lady! We liked that addition, and so did our patients. Great thinking on the part of these four wonderful men.

After bowing out of doing ultrasounds, I was asked to take the responsibility of doing hospital rounds and, initially, scrubbing for some cesarean sections with our doctors as they phased out the scrubbing duties at the hospital.

For years it had worked well to have another nurse do this, as the doctors used to go between two hospitals and liked to take their own instruments. The nurse would clean and re-sterilize them for use for the next case and bring them to the surgery suite. Over time, though, the doctors chose to use the hospital instruments and the hospital staff, and they decided to only practice at one hospital. They wanted me to make the rounds in that hospital, following up with patients there and occasionally at home.

The nurse who had done this job for years was very upset, but the doctors held firm. They requested that I handle the responsibility, so I did. Shortly after, the nurse quit, which made us all unhappy. She knew about all aspects of the practice, and we felt her loss keenly.

Eventually, between doing the extra duties, occasionally working longer hours than the normal 8:00–5:00, and having my husband working lots of overtime, I decided that I needed to give up my job at the office. It was time to take a breather from work and decide what my next steps should be. Our children were getting into more and more activities. We also had a property to manage in addition to our own home, and on weekends I drove two or more hours to and from it in order to take care of it, often without my husband.

I also felt the doctors needed more of a business manager than a nurse manager. When they laughed and told me I was working myself out of a job, I agreed. I was. They understood, though; they saw the need to align their practice with an experienced medical business professional who could help them get billing and other functions computerized. The medical-legal climate was getting more intense, and we all recognized that high-risk practices such as OB-GYN needed to have all their ducks in a row and the right people in the right jobs.

I think this was when I began to suspect that I should gain more credible knowledge about the business of healthcare. I had no doubt that healthcare could be delivered professionally while still maintaining ethical and appropriate business practices. I was also beginning to understand what a big business healthcare really was in the whole realm of our economy. As we have heard in recent times, it now makes up at least one-sixth of our GDP.

I did stay at the office per diem to give them a hand in staffing when someone was sick or on vacation. I treasured my experience there; it was such an asset to be on the other side of patient care revolving around women soon to give birth. It gave me a clear insight into why OB doctors cannot just race right out of their offices when the L&D nurse calls to say, "We need you right now." And it helped the L&D nurses to know that when I fielded their calls, I knew exactly how they felt.

I enjoyed some other wonderful opportunities as well. Among them, I helped the doctors work out a plan to have one of them always on call for deliveries and emergencies. The on-call doctor would not be tied up with office duties and so would be readily available. I also assisted with the triage of potential labor patients when the doctors were called out on emergencies. I discovered that even a specialty office such as an OB-GYN can master the unknowns of labors and deliveries and other OB-GYN emergencies.

I loved learning more about gynecology! This job gave me such great insights into the many facets of women's health. That field will always be a passion of mine.

But with other parts of my life demanding more of me, it was time to consider what to do next. I really didn't have a clue. I just knew that I was tired of trying to balance work and family needs, and my family came first. So I decided to see what would happen if I simply took care of their needs.

So I "retired" for eight or nine months — and discovered that I could be even busier as a retiree than I was working full-time. The occasional days when I worked for the OB-GYN practice took up a day or two here and there. Then I started helping a few friends with sewing problems and somehow ended up with a small business. I altered people's clothes, made everything from skirts to prom dresses, and got paid for my services. I even had a receipt book! I also got in touch with the labor and delivery unit at Sparrow Hospital and decided I could work there per diem as well on whatever shift or hours they needed help.

Then there was the volunteering. Everyone knows that when you are not a working mom, you volunteer for whatever. I was no exception. I volunteered mostly at the middle school where our daughter was a student. I also assisted our local youth hockey teams with their fundraiser and ended up with a house full of Beich chocolate bars for the players to sell. My worst problem was setting a quota for how many chocolate bars I would eat to help them out. Talk about will power! I never understood how I managed to be in charge of these candy sales for several years, but it may have had something to do with liking that smell of chocolate permeating our house! With our son and daughter both playing hockey, I had double the reason to have more chocolate in our home. Oh boy!

I finally decided I was going in too many

directions, and I certainly did not see myself spending the rest of my working life sewing or working per diem here or there. So in late 1985, I applied for a position as assistant department head on the night shift in labor and delivery at Sparrow Hospital, where two of my friends were doing the other two shifts. I figured that nights would work out best with my busy children's school activities. Our son had started playing travel hockey, and other sports when he could on the rare off-season, and our daughter was also active with sports and musical activities. We were an on-the-go family — including my husband, whose frequent travels required me to be available often as the family transport.

So night shift it was. I worked Sunday through Thursday and was even able to condense that into four nights a week at one point. Although L&D has never been all that predictable a unit to staff, and early evening hours were often challenging. Many of the scheduled labor inductions were likely to be delivering then, so we had some overlapping shifts to cover those busy hours.

Eventually the shifts for assistant department heads expanded to twelve-hour days and nights, with four of us to cover all but one day a week. We often ended up working that extra day as well. It was an incredibly busy L&D unit averaging 350 to 400 deliveries per month. The good part was that a lot of RNs worked in it, and we covered each other's shifts so we could all meet our needs outside of work. The downside was, we often needed all of our RNs if not more. Once we were put on a hiring freeze, and that did not go over well. More high-risk patients, more deliveries, and growing percentages of high-risk care procedures had become the new normal, and we let it be known that our current workload did not call for a hiring freeze.

We also received many high-risk transfers from other hospitals in Michigan. We never turned anyone away. Moreover, during the next four years we added more of our own dedicated OB anesthesia providers, and they helped us handle the escalating anesthesia needs that came with the growing numbers of high-risk patients. Not all of our numerous patients presented imminent deliveries, either. Some came and went with various obstetric problems. They might stay a few hours, a few days, or even weeks. And of course they eventually delivered their babies.

The variety was endless; the work, never boring; the epidurals and scheduled procedures, never-ending. These were great years for me in learning new nursing skills and perfecting previous skills. My position also taught me about such areas as policy-making, risk management, human resource management, and damage control. I worked with some of the greatest nurses ever, and we produced an incredible amount of work night after night, day after day. We knew each other's strengths and weaknesses and we balanced them out. I had many occasions to train new nurses and always enjoyed that piece of my job. Whereas prior to this time, L&D usually never hired newly graduated nurses, the tide and availability of qualified nurses had waned, and we began to hire new graduates if they demonstrated the qualifications. From my standpoint, the criteria boiled down to a willingness to work hard and learn, as I knew the rest would come.

Most nurses know very quickly whether L&D is for them, as it is so specialized and requires intensive nursing care. Generic nursing skills just can't cut it on most nursing units any longer; you have to have in-depth training on any given specialty. L&D was no different. Doctors who specialize look for certain criteria in the various nursing units, too, and that was evident in L&D. Although we nurses had our favorite doctors, we aimed to please all. That was our guiding principle for taking great care of our patients. If we worked well with our providers, life was good even if it was exceedingly hectic.

Probably not one of us nurses was not in tears at some point during our L&D years, whether tears of joy, sadness, or even anger. When one of our patients experienced a devastating event, we put our heads down and cried right along with them even as we completed whatever tasks we had to do for them.

Every delivery validated for us that each life was special. We saw some of the same patients more than once, and they usually remembered their nurses. I even had the great honor of having a baby named after me once, and I received several soul-nurturing thank you notes which meant so much to me. I have saved them all.

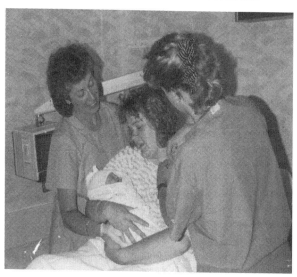

I wasn't the only one who learned a lot from

my L&D years. My family learned too, as they heard lots of "war stories." Our children also heard plenty about preventing pregnancy, especially after I had cared for a twelve- or thirteen-year-old young lady having a baby.

Before I left full time work in L&D at Sparrow Hospital in late 1989, I had switched to a staff position on the twelve-hour day shift in order to take a break from a management role. I was not sure that the overall management of our department was going well. I felt that what we needed were well-trained nurses to care for our patients, and I was up for being one of them.

We had become unionized by this time, which was not my preference. I had enjoyed far more success working with a team of nurses to solve any problems in labor relations, and I did not see how one union representative from our unit could speak for all our interests, no matter who that person was. In this regard, my sentiments were more on the management side; however, I would have been happy to help settle any issues from either side as long as both sides worked together.

After paying union dues for a few months and hating to see that amount leave my paycheck without any appreciable return on my investment, I chose to leave L&D and the hospital as well. Union representation for nursing was nothing I would ever care to support. Besides, a five-day weekday schedule would be better suited for the needs of my children. My husband was still traveling a lot and often unavailable to help with the children's activities later in the day. As much as I loved L&D nursing, I felt family needs far superseded having my first choice in nursing. I knew I could learn to enjoy other areas as well, though I chose to stay in women's health and continued to help out occasionally in L&D at Sparrow. I had begun a trend that lasted about twenty years: staying on more than one job in a per diem status so I could provide occasional assistance. I guess I have a hard time saying goodbye.

I took a job as charge nurse for the Ingham County Family Planning and Prenatal Unit and worked under one of the best leaders I have ever known in my nursing life. I was able to help with policy and protocol development, working closely with the director to start a quality assurance program, and learned a lot about regulatory compliance and how billing works in a publicly funded clinic. I began to learn a bit about the budget process, as my director discussed it with me. And I began to think about the master's program that my previous head nurse had completed through Western Michigan

University's Lansing Study Center. It was a public administration program that offered a healthcare concentration. I figured that if I were to be helpful in managing a clinic or department, I should know more about areas such as budgeting and organizational management, so I applied for the program and was accepted.

I have always been glad I made that move. What I learned was effectively in sync with great management for evolving healthcare entities. I was able to complete this fine program in four years, even with taking time off when other activities interfered. The program was designed to promote immediate application to one's current work situation, and it has been a great asset to me, starting with my job at the Ingham County Health Department.

In addition, the clinic offered me an opportunity to obtain certification as an OB-GYN nurse practitioner. Upon completing the condensed course, which was offered in another state, I would be required to work in the clinic as a nurse practitioner. But I had already considered going into nurse midwifery and decided against it; I felt the role was too limited, and I did not want to do home deliveries. The world of an OB-GYN nurse practitioner struck me as similarly limited and likely to restrict me to clinics or an OB-GYN office. So I declined the course. I did not want to abandon my family for several months to pursue something I wasn't sure I wanted to do. My decision fell opposite my usual behavior of taking a job when asked to do so, but it was the right choice for the right reasons.

I worked at the clinic for a year and am somewhat sorry that I left it so soon. But my reasons for doing so were clear to me. Having experienced the high-risk, high-volume, fast-paced life in labor and delivery, I found that I missed that kind of energy and care setting. More than anything, I longed for that level of patient interaction. I began to realize I would never be happy in any management position unless I could have quality patient contact — or, as I've often put it, "keeping my hands in it."

I applied for a director position in an OB unit at Hayes Green Beach Hospital, a small hospital in Charlotte, Michigan. I was offered the position and accepted it, eager to try my hand at managing a hospital nursing unit. The position met my hands-on nursing care needs, as I was the staff nurse every Wednesday for the twelve-hour day shift.

What followed was a tremendous learning experience and many hours at work, usually on shifts I could not otherwise fill. At the time I took this position, the unit did around 100–110 deliveries a year, but we did the labor, deliveries, and antepartum and postpartum care all on the same small unit, and ran the nursery there as well. It helped that I was familiar with the whole gamut of obstetric care, having worked in postpartum, helped in the nursery, and also had office experience in prenatal care. I was happy to be doing it all in one small department.

We worked mostly with family doctors doing the deliveries. Even our cesarean sections were usually performed by a family physician surgically trained to do them. These were experienced, credible practitioners, and I greatly enjoyed working with them. We had an OB-GYN or two from Sparrow Hospital on call, so occasionally I saw an old friend as well.

Hayes Green Beach certainly wasn't the kind of pace I had been used to, but just because it was a Level 1, low-risk OB provider hospital did not mean that high-risk patients never entered into our unit. Sometimes they literally dropped off the nearby highway presenting with various problems, such as severe preeclampsia, placental abruption, or the like. More often than not, just one RN was on the OB unit. That presented some problems during emergencies, sudden influxes of active labor patients, and other high-pressure situations.

As I was expected to be there five days a week, usually for eight-hour days, I was occasionally on the unit doing other administrative work without any patients on the unit. The RN scheduled for that shift probably either floated to the medical-surgical unit or was on call at home. In the early 1990s, we used LPNs primarily for the nursery, and they also cared for the postpartum patients. When there were no labor patients, which was most of the time, then the LPNs could staff the unit as RNs were readily available to us from one floor below on the medical-surgical unit. All our staff nurses on the OB unit were used to working the medical-surgical unit and had excellent clinical skills. If an RN wasn't already present when a labor patient came in, then the LPNs could put an external fetal and uterine monitor on a patient while the RN was on her way in or reporting off on patients downstairs prior to returning to OB. A great deal of trust and collegiality existed between the staff on this small OB unit. They worked very well together, and I loved that.

What was not so great were the frequent holes in the schedule that I just could not fill, even though all the nurses helped out when they could. They were used to scheduling needs, probably too used to them. Even — perhaps especially — in a small, more rural hospital, there was a lack of staff. I was the last option for an unfilled shift, and I covered it. Since I lived more than a half-hour away from the hospital, I had to be on the unit. Other labor RNs could stay at home on call provided they could be on the OB unit within a half-hour, as another RN in the hospital (usually the house supervisor) would cover until they arrived. I spent a lot of time on the unit — often getting a lot of administrative work done but also doing the nursing work, which I never minded.

What I did mind was that, in various ways, my family was showing signs of stress. Our children were teenagers, with all the usual teenage activities and issues. If they needed me, I was forty-five minutes away and often could not leave. I spent more than one twenty-four hour period on the unit rather than at home. My husband still travelled some, so occasionally he was not at home either. Having two teens at home alone did not create a comfortable situation. Not that our kids were bad, but they did have the usual tendencies all teens have at times — so sometimes my chief worry was that I wouldn't know when I should be worried! The situation just did not feel right. Not at all.

I was also working on my master's degree, applying for an army reserve nurse commission, and watching the world condition as the 1991 Gulf War began. I was very uneasy about the threat I saw brewing in the Middle East, and my interest renewed in serving as an army reserve nurse. I had first looked into army reserve nursing when I was thirty-four but found that the cut-off age for RNs at the time was thirty-five. That struck me as strange. Nurses who got their start in their twenties would have a lot more experience after ten to fifteen years of practice; they could increase their value to the military if allowed to apply when thirty-five or older. The army apparently recognized this too, because it raised the age limit for entering the Army Reserve Nurse Corps to age forty-seven. Now that, I thought, made great sense: the army could definitely benefit from more experienced nurses.

I began the process of applying for a commission at age forty-two. To my amazement, it took two years to complete all the requirements. At age forty-four, I was commissioned as a 1LT in the Army Reserve Nurse Corps — finally! I was so proud and so pleased that I could begin service with this proud group of nurses. What made it even more special to me was that I could share my news with my dad just a week before he passed away. His daughter was finally in the army, as he knew I had always wished to be. He told me that he was proud and happy for me, and that he knew I would serve with honor. I will always treasure that tenderly uttered compliment my dad gave me. It meant so much to me then, and it still does now.

Knowing that no relief was in sight for my overextended hours at the hospital in Charlotte, in February of 1992 I left to work in labor and delivery at a Level 2 hospital back in Lansing. Saint Lawrence Hospital was only twenty to twenty-five minutes from home, and an old friend from my Sparrow Hospital days — a nurse in the neonatal intensive care unit at the time — was now the department manager for this OB-GYN department. She hired me in.

Being part of a larger staff, without so much responsibility, brought me immediate relief. It was the right decision, though I did stay on per diem at Hayes Green Beach, picking up an occasional shift to help them out.

Like Hayes Green Beach, Saint Lawrence Hospital ran women's health as a department, but the various units were on two different floors. Labor and delivery was on the first floor right next to the emergency room and operating room. The postpartum, nursery, and gynecology units were on the second floor.

There was not a lot of floating between the different units, as most nurses liked working in one specific area. The nursery and postpartum nurses helped each other out more frequently than the L&D nurses. The L&D nurses were no sold on helping postpartum or nursery, and they usually got their wish to stay in the L&D unit, although sometimes, if it wasn't busy, they were put on call at home.

We had a Level 2 nursery also, for newborns that were more at risk than most normal newborns and needed various treatments such as intravenous antibiotics. I was handling all three levels of OB nursing care at this point, as I was still helping out at Sparrow Hospital L&D (Level 3) on rare occasion, and also Hayes Green Beach (Level 1). In most respects the level mattered not at all; higher acuity patients presented at all three levels.

Within a few months, the department manager asked if I would apply to be her assistant department manager, as the current manager had resigned. Since I didn't have to change my hours, I agreed. I took on the payroll functions and helped with policies, performance improvement, and other aspects of the labor and delivery end of our department.

We had LPNs or scrub techs on our shifts in L&D, and they usually scrubbed for cesarean sections and helped with L&D admissions and deliveries, mostly scrubbing in with doctors. But the LPNs also wanted do labor and delivery care. I listened to them, and we got approval to cross-train them to do labor and delivery nursing, which they did beautifully over time. We also began to cross-train some of the postpartum and nursery nurses to do labor care, but did not make it mandatory. We had a few willing participants, which was good for staffing flexibility.

Every job I ever took had its challenges, and this one was no different. The biggest challenge came from the historical impact of the OB-GYN providers on how our nursing department was run. Physicians understandably are required to be in charge of medical practice policies and practitioners, but I did not understand why they had much say in which nurses got hired, promoted, or fired. When they complained about a nurse, that nurse might not be with the department much longer. I found myself going to bat for a nurse or two as well as helping to define the role of nurse managers in supervising and doing performance improvement for nurses.

Things improved when physicians saw that our department was serious about taking care of nursing issues, but it was an uphill battle. During my three years at this hospital, I came to realize that I would always fight for nursing to take care of its own; the performance bar was ours to set and performance issues ours to manage. In my forty years of nursing, I have rarely worked with a nurse who did not wish to continually improve; I have; however, worked with many who raised the bar with their excellence in nursing practice.

My experience at Saint Lawrence Hospital strongly validated my belief that if we nurses and other healthcare providers worked as a team, we could work miracles with our patients and have great outcomes.

Chapter Five

Making a Difference

By early 1995, I had been a practicing RN for twenty-three years; I held a master's degree in public administration with a healthcare concentration; and I had been serving with an army reserve unit in Grand Rapids, Michigan, for about three years.

I also had two kids who were now in college. Our son was twenty-two and our daughter nineteen. Can I just say how proud I was — and am — of them? As I struggled to keep my body fat percentage within the allowed guidelines for my army reserve requirements, our son was working on getting his body fat percentage below 10 percent for a contest he was in at his college. I thought, Really? I could not imagine, but I could dream. Our daughter, petite little beauty that she was and is today, was working her way through college with the same great grade point she had throughout all her school years. Both today are success stories as parents and thriving beautifully in whatever they set their energies to do. I love them!

With the children on their own, at college and increasingly independent, I no longer had the concerns in 1995 that had surrounded so many of my earlier job decisions. My future in nursing seemed like it could go in any direction.

Maybe I didn't have to stay in OB nursing. My father's passing in 1992 had been an eye-opener for me, and I began to wonder about nursing care at the other end of the life cycle. Perhaps it was time to look at another field of nursing. I was restless, and I had become somewhat discontent with practicing in labor and delivery. Much of the spontaneity I loved was taken away by lots of scheduled labor inductions. Most women wanted epidural anesthesia, so options for pain relief had narrowed considerably with our labor patients. And overall, nursing care seemed always to be centered on procedures. Labors and deliveries were looking increasingly the same, and for a person wired like I am, that was becoming tedious.

Some of my nursing friends laughed at me and said things like, "Well, duh, Syl — of course it's the same all the time! It's always women having babies, one after the other." I had never felt like that was the beauty of L&D, though. For many years I had I thrived on the variety of labors and deliveries. But I no longer felt that way, even though I now recognized myself as one of those "motherly" nurses whom I had so admired for their great rapport with labor patients when I first started in L&D at age twenty-six. I believe I was also feeling the need for a challenge — to get out of my comfort zone.

I have never mentioned my husband's ideas or considerations for the jobs I have had. There is a good reason: he has never really had any. I have been blessed with the most supportive of husbands. If I even asked him for an opinion regarding options for a job, he simply shook his head and said that he didn't know what all the pluses and minuses would be, and I should do what felt best. Even when I said I was seeking a commission in the Army Nurse Corps, he raised no objections. What a guy — so easy to love this man!

I probably didn't discuss job possibilities or decisions much with our children until their teen years, when I was changing my working hours and positions to meet their activity needs. But I believe I had often shown them that I loved my work, however difficult it was. They and my husband heard a lot of my escapades at work and were amused by some of them — and perhaps appalled by a few others.

I once told our children that part of my love and willingness to work in addition to being a wife and mom was due to my own mother's regret that she did not work outside the home. My dad did not wish her to, and as I grew older, I could see that it affected her self-esteem. I never understood that, as I knew her to be an intelligent, wise woman regardless of whether she worked.

Only in more recent years have I recognized some of the negative feelings our children had about some of my jobs and my working in general. These feelings that come out in later years can hurt a lot for all parties. What to do with them?

I believe it helps to talk about them. Why might a child have felt anger or distress with a working mom? Had I known that my working was causing our children some angst, I probably would still have continued to work, but perhaps I could have better explained my choices to them when I was making job decisions. It might not have made a difference, but I would have at least tried to reassure them that they were always first with me. I would have wanted them to understand that my passion for nursing was something I felt called to do, but I would have also wanted them to know that my love for them was stronger still.

Other nurses have voiced a similar need to assure their families that working outside the home did not detract from their love of being a wife or mom. The struggle is common to our profession. Never are there enough nurses to meet patient care needs, and opting out of working means that one's workplace is short one more nurse.

I feel it is especially important to explain what

drives us to become nurses. For most of us, it is a heart for service. If your children and spouse can understand this even a little, they can better adjust to the time your job takes you away from them even as you try to maximize the time you spend with them. Hopefully, providing a role model of service can instill a similar heart in your children in a way that guides their own choices. (Of course, as they move into adulthood, they also need to understand their need to make an income!)

I have always felt that nursing is more of a calling than a job, and I believe my dad was happy that I picked nursing. He thought at one point that I wanted to be a social worker and was concerned that I would lose my shirt helping people. The nursing jobs I've written about in these pages were work, usually hard work, but I loved them because I love serving others.

That's why it was no stretch for me to serve as a military nurse. I have always viewed military service as necessary for our country's health, having been deeply influenced by my father. His service in the military stretched from his cadet status as a teen in 1918 to his retirement from the army reserves as a lieutenant colonel in 1954. He had a history that I loved and respected just as he loved it. My dad felt honored to have served. What a role model he was!

I wanted to not only serve with excellent civilian nurses, but also with the fine nurses in the military. I am blessed in having had the privilege to do both. There's a sign above the exit through the narthex in our church in New Mexico that says "Servants' Entrance." I have had many opportunities to look at it from where I sit in the choir loft. It expresses exactly what our faith expects of us: to pass through those doors, enter the outside world, and serve people. In my world, that's the right message no matter what one's faith is, and it describes how I have felt about my life's work.

I have not written of my nursing work as a career. That is no omission. I have never felt like I had or wanted a career. I have just wanted to take whatever opportunities came to me or those I particularly sought. Careers seem to me like planned, step-by-step movements toward some well-defined end. I have no idea what such a destination would be for me; it has been enough for me to just do whatever it is I'm doing at the moment. I can't even relate to retirement, nor do I have any idea when I might want to fully retire from nursing. It just doesn't sound like the right kind of thing to plan.

I have watched several physicians worry about when to retire. When I've talked with them, usually they didn't feel that they needed to retire at the time. I feel I'll know when it's time for me to fully retire. Economics of retirement have to be factored in; we would all like to retire when we can afford to. Then again, perhaps the decision will be out of my control.

The considerations that have shaped these later years in my nursing life have been different from those that influenced my earlier job choices. For instance, I need time to routinely see our grandchildren — and to golf as much as possible! Loving one's work does not make one a workaholic; many like me who love their work also love to play.

It was with an open mind that I took a position with Hospice of Lansing in 1995. As their nursing home coordinator, I spent most of my patient care time in nursing homes. I also helped with the coordination of other nursing home hospice teams in Michigan, as they were a relatively new component of hospice care. Most hospice care is done in-home, but not all hospice patients are capable of staying in a private home, and others do not have the caregivers needed to do so. I enjoyed providing the nursing end of hospice care and supporting the on-duty nurses who did most of the 24/7 physical care for the patients. Hospice nursing visits are brief visits only, to assess patient needs, provide treatments needed, and communicate needs to other players on the hospice team such as the attending physician, social worker, and chaplain.

There is a great sense of teamwork with hospice care. Teams usually meet weekly to report briefly on every patient's status, with all players attending and the meeting usually directed by either the hospice director or the hospice medical director. Occasionally other stakeholders — a pharmacist, for example, or a medical equipment provider — attend briefly for in-services or to provide special information, or perhaps to discuss a particular case in which they are involved.

To my surprise, moving from OB to end-of-life care was a smooth transition for me. The latter is an important part of the life cycle, and I found books written about the natural transition for OB nurses from labor and delivery care to hospice. I quickly found that I was very in tune with what my hospice patients needed for comfort care. Spur-of-the-moment needs were the ones I was used to meeting. So were exacerbation-of-care needs such as intractable pain. Hospice care was labor care of another sort, and it became a labor of love for me.

It felt good to support the nurses caring for our hospice patients in the nursing homes. They rarely saw doctors and often had a difficult time getting messages through to them, causing lapses in care needs which could be more promptly handled by the hospice team. The team could also work with some standard orders under the auspices of the hospice medical director. Many physicians chose to relinquish care to the hospice medical director, thus simplifying the process for obtaining needed orders. We were even able to bring a patient back home occasionally if they wished, and help arrange for meeting their around-the-clock care, within their resources. The social workers were very good at this.

Occasionally a patient inspired us by "flunking" hospice, as we called it: their life expectancy improved beyond the maximum of six months, and they were discharged from the hospice Medicare benefit. We recertified patients regularly to ensure that we were providing hospice care for those who continued to meet criteria. Of course, medical prognoses are not an exact science, and patients sometimes rallied or hung on to life longer than expected. So we carried many patients longer than six months if they met criteria. The hospice benefit is a wonderful benefit, and knowing that only so many healthcare dollars were available for it, we were committed to applying it as designed, validating every patient's eligibility.

In caring for hospice patients, I began to see an even broader scope for home care. I was occasionally able to have one of my nursing home hospice patients discharged to their own home or that of a loved one. Sometimes they had brief stays at a hospital-based hospice unit for pain or symptom management. These hospice units were designed to be home-like and comfortable for the patient and loved ones. But the locations weren't the only variable; there were the patients themselves, some of whom, as I have mentioned, were discharged from hospice care because they were expected to live longer than six months. Their care needs didn't simply disappear at that point.

During my year with Hospice of Lansing, I began to see a big black hole that too many people fell into, especially the elderly. They were not sick enough to be hospitalized, but they still had nursing care needs that needed to be met in order for them to stay at home and remain independent. The population over eighty years of age was and still is the fastest growing segment in our country. So I decided that I would like help manage people's nursing care in their own homes. I did not want to give up hospice care, but I also wanted to give others hope that they would not soon be hospice patients.

To this end, in 1996 I took a position as

education coordinator with a privately owned organization called Care Unlimited, Inc. My job was to make sure doctors knew that their homebound patients could receive home care for skilled nursing needs. I also visited different senior residences that asked for nurse speakers, routine blood pressure checks, or question-and-answer sessions regarding healthcare issues. This wonderful company was owned and managed by one of the finest people I have ever known — a businesswoman who had put her whole heart and soul into this operation, including much of her own resources. She is one of my heroes as she truly had a heart to serve the needy elderly and infirm in their own homes.

Working with the owner and another lead professional nurse, I helped develop programs such as quality assurance, determined next steps in home care development, and looked to the future to anticipate potential home care needs. It was a wonderful job, working together with dedicated professionals and also helping to train other nurses for various procedures in patients' homes.

I even helped with the transition when the company was purchased by a larger, nationally based home care company. Home care was under attack from insurers and the government, and smaller companies lacked the financial backing to continue their services to communities. That was a dark time in home care and for the elderly and infirm who needed home care services.

We found that a few bad apples could ruin home care for many. Several instances of fraud in Medicare billing were found in states such as Florida and Texas, as well as other states with high and growing populations of senior residents. Home care businesses popped up like ant colonies, and some were billing for services they did not provide. As a result, home care patients all over the country found their services in jeopardy. Reimbursements were cut, staffing shrank to the fewest possible workers, and authorization for home care visits became harder to get. From a nursing care standpoint, the situation was horrendous. Many people would not have good outcomes without skilled nurses checking on them for any of numerous reasons.

For example, a patient might need two months of home visits for wound care, yet the hospital discharge planners could authorize only one or two visits from a home care agency. At the same time, hospital stays were also coming under harsher scrutiny, with defined timelines for various diagnoses. Doctors had to define and redefine why any given patient might need to stay longer than allotted, explaining medical rationale to non-medical clerks. It was a bleak time in home healthcare, and it also contributed to the demise of many smaller hospitals which were not acquired by a larger hospital system. Communities suffered.

With the two professional leaders I had worked with regrettably out of the picture following the company's purchase, I stayed for several months to try to ensure that our preexisting patients were taken care of. Then I began to look for a role in home care with more of a future to it. I hoped to use my experience to help home care survive the Medicare cutbacks, and I wanted to encourage physicians to use home care for their needy patients.

During this time, one of my mentors from my master's program contacted me. Would I like to apply for the doctorate program in public administration, which was being offered again through Western Michigan University's Lansing Study Center? I pondered this for a while, wondering why I would need a doctorate. I had become fond of my educator role in home care. Perhaps a doctorate could give me a future in teaching or help me solve Medicare problems. I applied and was accepted into the program.

Again, I was simply doing what someone had asked me to do. My first term began with the obligatory two classes. That was the pattern for this doctorate, no exceptions: two classes each term, so the program could be completed in minimal time. That sounded good at the time — but I came to wonder about my sanity!

At least I no longer had childcare worries. Both children were out of college. Our daughter was married and our son was independent and working. Just my husband, two horses, a dog, and a cat were at home. But besides attending school, I was also drilling one two- or three-day weekend every month with my army reserve unit in Grand Rapids, Michigan, and attending its annual two-week yearly training. I was still filling in an occasional short shift in labor and delivery at one of my former hospitals. And in addition, in August 1998 I decided to accept a job as a director of clinical management for another home care company in the Lansing area.

Thus began one of the worst years in my nursing life. The company did well overall despite all the problems we faced, but I normally worked sixty to seventy hours a week and yet still never felt I had finished my work when I went home. The only nights when I left right at closing were the ones when I had my two three-hour doctoral classes.

Never before or since have I held a job with so many problems, and most of them began long before I took the position. To be fair, the regional director who interviewed me shared that some touchy issues were still being handled, so I was warned. I accepted the position mainly because the company dealt with private-duty home care as well as insurance-based home care, whether through Medicare or another insurer. The company also was willing to trial some disease management contracts, which interested me greatly. I have long taken a proactive nursing care approach to prevent problems before they have a chance to start.

Unfortunately for this company, and certainly for my role, the problems were various and abundant: personnel problems, irate patients and families, and staff who declined to care for some patients. It was an at-will agency, so nurses and aides did not have to take assignments, and there were several cases that nobody wanted to cover. I guess no one was hungry enough to take them, even with begging and pleading. Whatever the reasons, we could not meet the orders for care for some of our patients. We had to discharge them as we could not fulfill their care needs. That felt awful to me!

Clearly, something had to change. My first change was to drop out of my doctoral program after the first year. In the words of one of my favorite mentors, "Sylvia, it was just too much sugar for a nickel." This, too, felt awful, as I have never been a quitter, but I was not doing that well in one of the classes I was taking, so leaving seemed like the best option. My mentor said he knew I would finish my PhD when the time was right. I am sure I doubted his prediction, but it proved right years later.

My second step was to discuss leaving the job with my husband. I saw no end to many of the problems it posed. I didn't think it fair to him that I could never be home until late at night, only to return very early the following day. And I believed I was shortchanging the rest of my family by my continued service to this company.

Again my husband told me to do what I thought best, so I did resign — not, however, before finding a replacement job that was a complete change of pace. I left the company on my terms at a time when I felt I had solved many of its problems. I never willfully burn bridges, and this was no exception.

Chapter Six

Go Army!

While working for the home care company, I was putting in sixty to seventy hours a week, and my doctoral classes and studying took up any spare time I had. There were no free weekends to do much of anything, including spending one weekend a month in Grand Rapids for drills. So I changed my army reserve status to Irregular Ready Reserve (IRR). I still had to complete annual trainings, and I fulfilled that commitment.

But I really missed the camaraderie, learning, and great experiences I had while drilling with my reserve unit. I had accomplished a lot of training in the seven years I had been associated with this medical unit, and had even managed to pass all my PT (physical training) tests twice a year! My army commitment was good for my soul, training me to be of service to my country whatever the need might be and also enhancing my nursing skills.

Soon after I received my commission as a first lieutenant, I attended officer basic training in San Antonio, Texas, at Fort Sam Houston. That was truly a "you're in the army now" experience, validating my decision to serve with this productive branch of the military. We learned a lot about soldiering during those two weeks, and

I met a lot of soldiers who were as glad as I was to be a part of the army reserve.

It was a decent time to be in San Antonio, as the two weeks started at the end of November and ran into December. We got to see the River Walk decorated for Christmas while enjoying the mild San Antonio weather.

An added benefit to the officer basic training was my roommate, who had been an enlisted service member prior to getting her commission as an army reserve nurse. She had a good comfort zone with all things military. After hearing about her escapades working in the emergency room of a hospital in downtown Los Angeles, where she had to physically defend herself on more than one occasion, I felt like I had great protection! Our commanding officer cautioned us to never go out alone in San Antonio; we were told to always go with at least one other person, or preferably a group. We took those precautions to heart, as soldiers were often targeted for holdups, especially on their widely known paydays.

Some new officers were even older than I was at age forty-five. One gung-ho anesthesiologist told us she was sixty-five and had always wanted to be in the army. She was as eager as the rest of us to experience it all. She did have difficulty with our military boots, however, and ended up in the emergency room at Brooke Army Medical Center with sores on her feet, some of which got infected. She was plucky, though. She did what she could, and I have often wondered if she was able to serve as she wished to.

At the time I received my commission, the cutoff age for army reserve nurses was forty-seven. One of my best friends who joined the reserve unit in Grand Rapids just prior to my start was actually forty-seven when she received her commission, narrowly making the deadline. She and I had a great time during the seven years we drilled together, and we are still friends today. We stayed in Grand Rapids during our monthly training weekends, as we both lived too far away to travel back and forth, and we even studied together at night. She was working on her nurse practitioner degree and I was finishing my master's around the time we started, and I began my doctorate four years later.

Officer basic training taught us all kinds of skills, from recognizing the various army vehicles, aircraft, and tanks, to getting in and out of protective gear (MOPP gear) in fourteen seconds. I met the required timing for the MOPP gear, but in repeating the procedure multiple times, I ended up with costochondritis (sore rib cage) from my flashlight poking me in the right rib area when I bent down to pull on the boots. I actually was sent to the post hospital's emergency room because the rib area was so painful that I had a difficult time taking a deep breath. No breaks, just soft tissue injury and a good lesson learned: don't keep anything on your person that can stab you in all the wrong places and injure you.

That experience put a damper on my partying at our last event together as a group. But other successes compensated. I qualified with the pistol, a 9mm Beretta. And I managed to find my way out of some far-away field using a compass, so I didn't stay lost in the territory around San Antonio. I didn't meet any snakes, either — another success!

My husband was always relieved when I came home from any weapons training. The first time I went, he seemed agitated, and his last comment as I walked out the door was, "Just come home alive." I do believe he was concerned about Syl having anything to do with a weapon! He need not have worried. Since I had zero experience with firing any weapon, I paid strict attention to all instructions — especially about the safety features. I also parked myself next to a nice young man who had taken apart, cleaned, and put a weapon back together again more times than he could count, so when we were taxed with that bit of training, I looked and learned, and he corrected me as needed. As I have already noted, I'm not blessed with much mechanical ability; I have to do something over and over again to know how to operate any piece of equipment, screwdrivers included.

But in the military, there are people always willing to help and teach. You have only to open your mind, ears, and eyes to benefit from the expertise around you. I followed the same principle in putting up our medical units, tents, and the like: I just followed someone who knew what they were doing. I'm good at that. I also know how to take orders and follow, which is darn useful, both in the army and out!

What was so clear to me in the military was that military personnel always appear to understand the mission, and they know that any one order is just one small part of that mission. I cannot say the same about many civilian work situations; there is often a confusion of purpose and probably a whole lot of selfishness. In the military, there is a stronger sense of pulling together. I would submit, though, that civilian work situations can foster the same consensus, and those are the work environments I have always chosen or at least tried to develop.

A few years later, officer advanced school gave me more of what I got in officer basic training, only in greater depth. The bad part was going back to San Antonio in July, as it was hot — no, it was really hot! I was grateful I had already done my PT testing for the current six-month period, as I would not have relished getting out in the swampy atmosphere at four or five o'clock in the morning and running or even walking. I did exercise, however. The university where we were staying had an Olympic-sized pool, and while it felt like bath water, it surely beat running in that hot, humid weather.

We didn't actually get to Ft. Sam Houston very often as most of our classes were at the university. We didn't have much field training either. Most of our training was through texts and classroom lectures. I even had time to go with a couple of the officers to play a round of golf at the air force base, but the only tee time we could get was at 2:00 in the afternoon in incredible heat. I think the men drank about six Gatorades apiece. I stuck to water and was fine, but we all questioned our sanity for golfing in 116-degree heat. We had fun, heat and all. Soldiers know how to work hard, but they also know how to have fun together. I believe this is why many stay in the military. It is a family.

My unit in Grand Rapids had some fun annual trainings too. We were a backfill unit for Ft. Gordon in Augusta, Georgia, and held two of our annual trainings there during the seven years I drilled with the Grand Rapids unit. One year we were scheduled during the Masters Golf Tournament, but I had no luck getting to see any of that! The surgeons at Dwight David Eisenhower Medical Center had better luck with tickets for the Masters, and the surgical volume definitely shrank during that time!

I worked on a surgical unit during one of the Georgia trainings, and in ambulatory surgery the next time, but I still found a little time to use my golf clubs. My friend and I drove down from Michigan so we could have a car, and that enabled us to take a couple side trips — once to Charleston, South Carolina, and the next year to Savannah, Georgia. Our commanders ensured that we had some play time during these trainings.

In the army, I worked with some of the finest professionals in my experience. The clinical expertise of many of our unit's members ensured that we had critically needed training in many areas of clinical practice. Our critical care nurses were second to none. We were fortunate to have them teach a course which included hands-on training at a local hospital in the emergency room and the intensive care unit. We put our learning to work for the community, and it was appreciated. The critical care nursing certification I received was put to good use years later when I worked in the ER of a busy downtown hospital.

We participated in various kinds of training covering multiple specialties in different facilities around the Grand Rapids area. We also learned how important dental health was in military planning, as well as the key role that psychiatric care played in military health initiatives. Our medical unit had plenty of specialists as well as an occasional family doctor and various surgeons. We did not have a veterinarian, but that profession did not get overlooked. Various animals serve in the military, and they receive the care and training they deserve.

We had our own chaplain, too, so we had the opportunity to attend a brief, non-denominational church service on Sunday mornings. It was clear to me that the military was a family, with no role or activity overlooked. We even had lunch breaks! We had it all, with superb professionals committed to a cause far greater than any one individual. We were a team, and we felt privileged to be a part of it. It was not easy to leave this fine unit when I transferred to irregular ready reserve status in 1999 due to the time constraints caused by my work and advanced-degree schooling. Still, modifying my level of service was acceptable. But abandoning my commitment to serve as long as I could was never an option.

I had a few other memorable two-week annual training sessions during my earlier army reserve years. At Ft. Carson in Colorado Springs, I worked in a labor and delivery unit, which was fun and low-key. I drove myself from Michigan to Colorado, as I wanted my car available, and because I had invited my mom, who had by this time been a widow for eight years, to come out to visit close family friends in the Denver area. She did so the second week of my training.

Between work shifts in the hospital, my mom and I did some sightseeing and visited our friends. I was so glad I had included her; it was the last time she would see these friends.

My time in the army gave me opportunity after opportunity, not only to serve the American people in numerous ways, but also to enjoy the many benefits of traveling to different states and even countries. I once had the opportunity to go to Germany on a voluntary assignment. Due to family concerns, I regretfully declined, but it was nice to have been given the chance.

While at Ft. Carson, I had to do a training assignment of my choosing. I chose to research and give a talk on customer service. That was a topic I felt any nurse could easily prepare and deliver, with great examples of what worked and what didn't. Of course, the word customer never seemed to fit the patients we serve in healthcare, but the premise of good service was the same. It is about meeting or exceeding customer needs and ensuring that the customer is part of any decision making. Service is at the core of the military, but I had some fun in putting a lot of spin on it from the civilian side as well. That is something for which we reservists are known — taking our military learning to the civilian sector. I knew I could utilize my research in any job in my civilian life as well. In future jobs, I worked key concepts of customer service into orientation with any new employee I trained.

In March of 2000, I was given the choice of going to Ft. Lewis in Tacoma, Washington, or Tripler Medical Center in Honolulu, Hawaii. That's a choice? Off to Tripler I went, though at one point I thought the plane was taking me to Ft. Lewis because its flight pattern passed over Washington State. I thought it more likely we would be flying over Los Angeles. Instead, I got to see an unforgettable sunset over Mount Hood and Mount Rainier. I took it as a good omen, and I was right — I had an incredible experience at Tripler.

What a hospital! The locals called Tripler the "Pink Palace," as the outer walls were a light pink stucco. It was a large and busy hub, with patients coming from all over the Pacific Rim. The army at that time had a computerized medical records and patient documentation system, allowing us to key directly into pertinent patient data with transfers from anywhere in the world. This was pretty neat, considering that many elements of today's civilian hospital culture are still far from having consistent computerized documentation or patient information data systems.

I worked on an antepartum floor at Tripler with

pregnant or newly delivered moms who required hospitalization for various problems. Pre-term labor problems were fairly prevalent, as was preeclampsia. Some mothers were hospitalized because they had an infant in the neonatal intensive care unit. It wasn't a very busy two weeks, and it seemed like we had a lot of help, but I paid attention to any differences in the treatment of maternal complications. Most treatments reflected what I knew to be the current standards of care, which was reassuring.

This time my husband flew out toward the end of my two week stint, and we flew to the "Big Island" — the one actually called Hawaii — and stayed a few days. That was a wonderful way to end an assignment, and I was grateful to my boss for making it possible. The army assignment was non-negotiable — I had to go and complete my two week assignment — but the extra time off from the civilian side was a gift, and greatly appreciated.

The army allowed me to hang on to my housing unit on post during our few days on the Big Island. That was not unusual for the military. They try to make accommodations for service members and their families as convenient as possible, and they bring families together when possible.

The next year's annual training in August 2011 took me to Fairbanks, Alaska, and Ft. Wainright. That will always rank as my very favorite annual training. I've seen eyebrows raise when I have said this. People can't imagine what is so appealing about a state that is mostly winter. But Alaska has a charm all its own — and of course, I was there in August, not December! The worst thing I had to put up with was black flies, which liked to come golfing with me.

I declined a "learning to drive in the snow" class — after all, I was from Michigan and had driven in snow all my life. Granted, Alaskans really get snow, but as they didn't think it would come for a few more weeks, I was probably safe without the training. Alaska has about two months of summer; it is winter the rest of the year. But that brief Alaskan summer is beautiful! I did my PT testing by myself with a proctor, running along a dirt trail among the whispering pines.

Once again I worked in OB, helping to birth those army babies, and totally enjoyed my time there. Our unit was equipped to do cesareans, a plus if needed. It was a fun staff, and we had some great deliveries. Army moms and wives took care of their own babies, and they did so long before "rooming in" hit the civilian sector. That was the expectation: healthy babies went out to be with healthy moms. However, those that were sick stayed in the nursery with specialized nurses most of the time.

 I worked with another reservist from Virginia, and we managed to get our schedules worked out together so we had some free days to sightsee. We went to Denali and actually saw the peak, a spectacle not all visitors get to enjoy as that magnificent mountain is often hidden in clouds. We also went whitewater rafting, which certainly was a highlight. I was only sorry that my husband could not join me. Like me, he would have enjoyed the area and the warm, wonderful native people. Maybe someday we will go there together. I figure that if there's no other way open for us to travel somewhere, I can always get a temporary nursing position there!

Chapter Seven

A Recovering Nurse

When I make a change, I make a change. When I left the home care company that was threatening to tie me in knots, I took a position as a human resources manager at the Radisson Hotel in Lansing. Yep — a non-nursing job, although it did have similarities to being a house supervisor at a hospital.

I was responsible for managing a lot of people I had never met, and I hadn't a clue as to what they did. It was a great job, and I had an amazing boss, the general manager of the hotel. I learned a lot about the complexity of hotel management during my year-and-a-half at this job, and certainly a lot about people.

My position as HR manager involved not only the traditional human resource tasks such as interviewing, hiring, counseling, and teaching orientation classes, but a lot of statistical and financial chores as well. I did a lot with payroll, working with tip reporting for the servers in the hotel, housekeeping, and other areas, and submitting the tip reports each pay period. I also sat in with the general manager on some personnel counseling and other issues; and I even trained to be a TIPS trainer — that is, an alcohol management trainer. That was a new role, but a very important one in ethical hotel/restaurant management.

I performed other duties as well which any nurse who reads her job description for a position would recognize. Remember that last line of job duties which said something like, "... and any other duties as assigned by your supervisor"? Let me tell you, in a busy downtown hotel, that can include a lot of variety. I learned how to control crowds in the lobby in order to maintain decorum, almost learned how to check people in or out of the hotel, helped fill salt and pepper shakers in the dining room, assisted with table clearing for banquets, and even tasted all the different chilis that our head chef made for an annual chili cook-off contest — all morning long, until I could no longer feel my tongue or lips!

I helped with reports of various kinds, ran a cigar room for a banquet, shooed unnecessary people out of the chef's kitchen a time or two before he exploded, learned that a sous chef does not want to be asked to make a batch of cookies (even when I asked nicely), and found that I had at least a little knack for the billing and financial considerations of the hotel. I came to a workable agreement with tipped employees that would please even the nastiest IRS type. I helped housekeepers when they were swamped, managed uniforms, and even took blood pressures now and then.

There were perks, of course, for all the hard and varied work, and that was nice, as I was salaried and worked far more hours than my job description called for. The biggest perk was that I enjoyed my work! But there were plenty of other benefits. My husband and I enjoyed a free dinner or two in our nice dining room. I participated in some hotel management seminars, and my boss was willing to teach me almost anything about how the hotel ran and the role our management company played. I got to see some famous people, among whom was my personal favorite, Barbara Bush, wife of the first President Bush, and a lady I have always admired.

My fellow workers and I even got treated to fancy cigars after a couple of the banquets. We would trot downtown when our work was finished to relax with a drink and smoke our cigars. There must be something intriguing about a lady smoking a cigar, as we attracted considerable attention from male patrons, not all of it desired. One drunken moron picked up the cigar I had put in the ashtray and proceeded to take a puff on it. I was vastly annoyed, and for sure I didn't pick it up again — though with the amount of alcohol on his breath, it might have been sterilized. Yuk!

And then came Y2K. In a hotel, that was a BIG deal. We did all the training, checked and double-checked all the parameters of the switchover on our computers, did various inspections of the systems that would be affected, and then just started to pray that all would go as planned. I don't think anyone anticipated that it would be as smooth as it turned out to be. My boss suggested (I think it was a suggestion) that I come in just before midnight and make sure all went as planned. Had something actually gone wrong, I'm sure I wouldn't have known what to do. But the night passed uneventfully.

Hotels are like that if they are well run: they anticipate any disaster, plan for it, and celebrate when it doesn't happen. My husband, on the other hand, was of the opinion that Y2K would do nothing more than come in as the calendar indicated. Such faith! He just went to bed. Smart man.

I was knee-deep in human resource functions when I began to realize that I really did miss nursing — not management, but giving care to patients. By then I was a certified hospitality supervisor. It sounded nice, and I had even received the distinction of achieving the second highest national employee satisfaction rating as an HR manager within our management company.

But I did not see how these things would carry me into the future.

My husband had retired from General Motors in 2000. Our daughter had moved to Virginia, and I felt that we needed time to see her and maybe take a vacation as well — more time than one or two weeks off a year permitted. So I decided to do the simple thing: find a part-time job and leave the Monday-through-Friday hotel week. I had not worked part-time in almost twenty years, and in many ways I hated to leave the hotel. I had a wonderful boss and great friends there. I had my recovery period, though, and was truly refreshed. Back to the basics of nursing for me, and it felt so right.

Back to Hayes Green Beach Hospital I went but this time as a part-time OB staff nurse on the twelve-hour night shift. The hospital was still strongly supported by its small community and appeared in good financial health. It was also affiliated, mostly in management, with a larger Lansing hospital. I was not worried that it would close.

I started to reorient in earnest in January 2001 and easily slid into a pattern of sixty hours per two-week pay period. It was a nice, workable schedule, and I loved this time of simply taking care of moms and newborns and reuniting with many of my friends from my director days. The department was doing more deliveries, but nothing like a busier Level 2 or Level 3 OE department. We had several OB-GYNs on staff by this time, though, and 24/7 anesthesia coverage, so we enjoyed many of the benefits of a higher-acuity OB department.

It felt great to be a staff nurse again! It was also great to not be the last woman standing and have to fill a shift no one else would take. To be sure, I filled in several shifts to help out when I could. The need to fill extra shifts has always existed in any hospital where I have ever worked. The only change now was, I was wise enough to at least start with a part-time work schedule.

I worked at this fine hospital until my husband and I took off on a truly life-changing path. In May of 2002, we sold or gave away most of our possessions, including our home, and left Michigan in our 36-foot motor home. We planned to travel wherever our hearts led us and eventually find a place we would love to call our forever home. We anticipated that it would probably be somewhere in the Southwest, but we were open to other options and to looking around wherever our curiosity led us.

Several months into our motor home journey, we found that our first instincts were right and that the Southwest would be our future. We had traveled to Kentucky, Tennessee, Virginia, and back to Michigan, where I picked up a couple shifts with the OB unit at Hayes Green Beach. had stayed on per diem at the hospital; however, I terminated that relationship in December, as by then we knew we would not be coming back to Michigan again except to visit our son. I also had started working for a hospital system as a part-time hospice nurse in Albuquerque, New Mexico, and the home we were having built was almost ready!

I had signed with a travel nursing agency when we left Michigan and taken a three-month contract at a small hospital in Taos, New Mexico, in August 2002 to work nights in their OB department. I figured I would take a couple three-month contracts a year to have a little extra money with which to travel about and to explore areas we wanted to see in depth. We picked New Mexico for my first contract, as we had always wanted to explore that state. A nursing friend had gone to New Mexico for a week or two each year for many years and praised the beauty of this Land of Enchantment. We were not disappointed. We fell in love with New Mexico from the time we first drove into it that August. Within a month or two, we were signing paperwork to have our home built in Albuquerque and convincing my mom to come live with us. She had been very lonely back in Michigan since my dad had passed away in 1992, and I also suspected her health was not as good as I would have liked.

Our home was built in record time, and my mom was able to sell hers quickly as well. By December 2002 we were all back in Albuquerque waiting for the house to have its finishing touches completed. My husband and I stayed in our motor home; my mom, temporarily in a hotel.

I found a job quickly, knowing that we would now be supporting two homes — our new permanent home and our home on wheels. I took a position part-time with Presbyterian Hospice to do outpatient hospice in patient homes, and I also worked a shift here and there in the hospital inpatient hospice unit as well. I was pleased to be in hospice again and worked with a great hospice team, from the bottom up and top down.

We moved into our home in northwest Albuquerque in January 2003. My mom let my husband and I settle in first, then moved in with her furniture a few weeks later. We got off to a great start. My job usually had me home no later than two o'clock. I did not have to work every weekday, and I did not usually work any weekends. My mom joked that she had finally gotten through with all her ablutions and minor chores and was ready to sit down and read or write letters and visit with me by the time I got home. My husband even started to look for a part-time job.

We were on a nice roll, all getting used to living together in our home, when the orders came for me to report to Walter Reed Army Medical Center.

Just a note here to put my time at Walter Reed in perspective. I've already shared how much this service to our country meant to me. In the whole scheme of my nursing life, I was tossed challenges of one sort or another, and my experience at Walter Reed, ranking as one of the most meaningful times in my life, was a huge one.

There is never really a good time in life to be handed such challenges, just a time when a person knows they have to kick themselves into an extra gear they never knew they had. To anyone who cares to listen: one should embrace these challenges. They can brighten your world in so many ways. My family and I got through it, and life went on, and we all came to a deeper recognition that even when we were apart, we shared a bond that could not be broken.

Chapter Eight

And Beyond...

I left Walter Reed knowing that my PhD in health administration was done, over, finished! My dissertation had been approved, my requirements completed, and once all the paperwork was submitted, my degree would be in the mail to my home in New Mexico. I ever had the opportunity to present a brief summation of my dissertation to the combined nursing staff at Walter Reed. I did my dissertation on nursing retention; it was specific to hospitals in New Mexico, but the principles behind effective nursing retention could be applied in any setting. It was an honor to be asked to talk about this subject to our nursing staff at Walter Reed.

I had to print my dissertation yet again when I got to our son's home in Michigan, and he recently reminded me that I pretty much did in his printer. I made up for it in childcare, though, when I got to Michigan — after I had slept. When I first arrived at my son's home in Portage, Michigan, I slept a long time. (How does one make up for fifteen months of active duty?) I was making the transition from army nursing to helping with a newborn, and a preemie at that. Our first grandchild — what a thrill!

The 24/7 infant care cycle came right back to the forefront of daily life, as if it had never been missing for the last twenty-eight years. I could not believe how thrilled I felt to be a part of our first grandchild's life and be able to help out. As any preemie would, he had to eat often around the clock to gain some weight. We settled into a routine that was comfortable to us all, and my part was babysitting and feeding Brendan after his mom went to bed. Usually my son was awake and helping up until eleven o'clock, but then he had to go to bed so he could get up for work. I had Brendan all to myself until around 3:00 a.m., when I laid him, sound asleep, in the cradle beside his parents' bed. Then I conked out. Did I love that time to have the little munchkin all to myself? You bet — food not only for a grandma's soul but a nurse's soul as well! I helped Brendan get a jump start, and his parents some sleep.

Soon it was time to go home to New Mexico — at last. I had been gone about seventeen months, and boy, was I ready to revive my New Mexico life. First things first, of course, and that was my job, but only after spending some quality time with my husband and mother and finding places to put my gear. That was no mean feat. My husband and mom had managed to fill up the house, and there was not as much room as I remembered.

I realized that working part-time was no longer an option. I needed full-time at this point, although my husband was now teaching at a business school full-time. Unfortunately, although Presbyterian Hospice gave me back my part-time position, they did not have a full time slot. So I began to look for other work while doing some outpatient hospice care. I tried various avenues looking for a rewarding position, but it eluded me for the next couple of years. Finally I figured out why.

For over a year I had invested so much of myself in the wounded warriors at Walter Reed, caring for so many and enabling their healing and recovery over months and months of hospitalization, that the shorter-term, visit-type work of hospice and the temporary shift work in local hospitals simply did not satisfy. I finally realized that I was not committed to any one line of work. So I signed on with a temporary staffing agency and worked some shifts here and there in local hospitals. I also obtained a per diem job at the Metropolitan Detention Center in Albuquerque. Now that was an education!

The shifts at the jail reinforced my belief that we never see it all; something will inevitably happen to open our eyes yet again, and some things are better forgotten as well. The inmates really liked the nurses, and they liked coming to the clinic with whatever complaint they could muster. Some complaints were obvious and treatable, such as the plastic spork one young man had stuck into his nether parts. I had never done that kind of wound care before the few months when I worked at the center — or after! Other complaints were less visible and more difficult for the inmates to define, so back to the pods they went, as they were symptom-free. But they continued to like the medical staff, even though we would not let them just hang out in the clinic.

Finally I got the full-time hours I needed working in Presbyterian's busy downtown ER. That was another eye-opening experience. I felt as if I was in a constant state of busyness that had no beginning and no end. I also felt that we did not meet anyone's needs — certainly not those of patients who got discharged with no real answers as to what might be wrong with them.

We made no friends when transferring patients in varying states of readiness to floors that were already overwhelmingly busy. Usually we had no choice, as we needed another ER bed for a patient coming in via ambulance. We surely didn't help our charge nurse, who was trying his or her best to handle the ER traffic. There was very little time to educate patients who were discharged, many of whom needed more treatment than we could give them. We tried to find primary care for many patients, referring them to various low-cost or no-cost clinics, but had little success. Many of the patients simply came back to ER again and again.

For several reasons, I left ER to become an RN office manager for a busy general surgeon's practice which was affiliated with Presbyterian. I still had not found what I was looking for and I knew it, but I temporized with my work, wanting to be available for my husband and mother as much as possible. My mother's health had begun to fail within a few months of my return to New Mexico in the summer of 2004. She had a mild heart attack as well as notable confusion, which precipitated a progressive mental decline, and she ended up in the hospital and its geriatric rehab center for several weeks. When we were about to start living together in Albuquerque, my mom and I had discussed what would happen if she needed more care than I could comfortably deliver in our home; we now revisited that discussion.

My mom always clearly desired not to be a burden to anyone; she would rather take care of others than be taken care of herself. However, her needs at this point did not lend themselves to allowing her to be without any nursing help, so when she finally came home from the rehab center, she required occasional care from a visiting nurse. That was awful for us both. She hated having others come into our home; yet, neither did she really want me waiting on her or trying to arrange my work schedule around her needs. The visiting nurse lasted long enough to ensure my mom was at a stable point, with no further heart damage occurring. I was home for every visit of the nurse, as that helped my mom be at least somewhat more comfortable and accepting of the nurse's services.

A word here for nurses who believe they will always be able to meet the needs of loved ones and who would prefer to personally provide whatever nursing care is required: doing so takes mutual consent, and even then, either you or your loved one may change your mind. Especially when dementia is a factor, determining care parameters for the elderly can be difficult. In my opinion, the care decision should be as mutually acceptable as possible, and if any errors are to be made, they should be on the side of your loved one's safety and well-being.

When it became evident that my mom needed to be around people more of the day, she and I discussed how that could happen. There were two ways. The first option was to have home health aides or companions assist in our home during weekdays. The second option was for her to move to an independent living situation where she could take her lunch and dinner with others and only have to fix her own breakfast in her apartment. She opted for the latter; she was not about to have those people in our home again. We found her a wonderful place — she even voiced that she liked having her own place again, and we shopped for some new furniture for her, which delighted her.

Such are the decisions we all may have to face at some point with a family member. In my mom's case, she was not a happy person in her later years. With Alzheimer's progressing, she was not the mom we once knew, and the dementia added to other problems. When a minor surgery sent her to a nursing home to recover, I was unable to get her back to her independent living apartment. She knew that nurses would have to enter it, and she wanted no part of that, or of trying to live on her own, or of "bothering" my husband and me.

When I tried to discuss options, I was met with a blank stare; my mother would not discuss the matter. The only thing I could do was get her a private room at the nursing facility. She was mostly pleased with that. She did not want to be with anybody else, yet she also hated being in a room by herself. It was a difficult situation all around, and one that grieved us all. We think we did what was best at different times, but who can really know? All I can say, if you're a nurse in a similar position with a relative, is to go with your gut and try to make your decisions as mutual as possible. Know yourself and know your limits; and, if you are married, consider your mate.

In August 2005, while still searching for a meaningful job, I took a three-month full-time contract with an outpatient hospice team that was in the process of being sold. That turned out just about right, as at the end of the contract I ended up back at Walter Reed to meet my military duties for annual training and drill requirements. I returned to Ward 57 for a split three-month duty and worked with many of my former coworkers and even some patients. Best of all, during that time came the birth of our daughter's first child — our second grandchild and first granddaughter.

I hung out with my daughter and son-in-law for the labor and delivery, which was an amazing and gratifying experience. Most OB nurses will affirm that every delivery is special in its own right. But the birth of your own child or grandchild — now that's really special! I was thrilled to help and to get my hands on precious little Christina right away. Since our daughter still lived handily nearby in the Washington, D.C., area, I was able to be with her during the end of her pregnancy and the beginning of motherhood. I have precious memories of the wonder and privilege of that time, including the way the army accommodated my family needs in the midst of my duties.

I completed my physical training in the winter of 2005, and I am elated that I will never again have to jog two miles around the veranda at Walter Reed on a frigid December day! I wondered if would ever be able to breathe again, as the air I was sucking in was so cold. But I lived through it, I finished, and I passed Amen. This three-month time was a wonderful reminder of the spirit and decency of our military, who have given us such great service.

It was also my last time to serve; I was honorably discharged at age sixty, as is the norm. My husband enjoys saying that I was probably the oldest nurse captain ever to serve in the army reserve, or at least the one who served as a captain the longest. That is an honor I will gladly take. I was just pleased that the army had made the correct decision to retain experienced nurses when the need was at an all-time high and did not discharge them simply because they lacked a bachelor of science in nursing.

Back in Albuquerque in early 2006, I decided to take a couple per diem jobs that appealed to me. A company with a New Mexico office in Albuquerque hired me temporarily to conduct HEDIS (Healthcare Effectiveness and Dat Information Set) audits. I went to various doctors' offices, hospitals, and clinics to review patients' charts for compliance with standards of care for various diseases such as diabetes. I enjoyed this work. It proved that the medical community by and large was doing what it should for its patients. The standards of care were not only met but usually exceeded, and with good documentation.

I also took a job as a house supervisor at a local hospital branch that was being absorbed by a bigger hospital in the area. I worked per diem here as well on varying shifts, mostly days, and also helped to transition out many of the departments and staff. The emergency room needs were among the most time-consuming. The ER was busy even though the hospital inpatient units were being gradually transferred out. It was the only ER on the far southwest side of Albuquerque, and it had a steady clientele.

There were other mentoring and staff support functions that I helped with as well. Transitions like this are never very easy on staff who have been at one facility a long time. The place is home to them.

These two jobs were good ones for me to have at the time, even though I felt that I was still coasting. But with the decline I saw in my mom, I was happy to be more available by having flexible schedules up until the summer of 2006, when I knew that my coasting had finally come to end. My temporary per diem jobs were finished and family finances were clear.

I completed a lot of job applications and interviews, as I wanted to get it right when I finally committed to a full-time job again. With my PhD in health administration, I figured I should have a job that could make good use not only of my experience but also my education. Whole Health Management in Cleveland, Ohio offered me just such a job. It was unique and interesting. The company had contracted with Intel Corporation to supervise the wellness program that Intel was starting at thirteen of its campuses, most of which were out west.

Working for Whole Health Management, I learned the wellness business from the ground up. We provided some basic lab draws and biometric services for Intel employees who wished to participate in the program, and we provided health coaching once the biometrics results were available. As the lead health coach, besides coaching, I also supervised the other twelve teams in Arizona, California, Oregon, Washington, Colorado, and Massachusetts. I travelled frequently to the various sites to meet different needs and attend management meetings and face-to-face meetings. There were a lot of phone conferences as well. My boss was terrific, and we hit it off well from the start. I was amused to know that he was half my age and right out of Harvard Business School.

It was a wonderful job in many respects. I was learning a new field and obtained my certification as a wellness coach — not a simple study by any means. Lots of work goes into the certification, and a person has to demonstrate what they know. I worked with some superb professionals with backgrounds in dietetics, personal training, yoga, various kinds of wellness training, and more. It was a privilege to work with this team and also with our local New Mexico Intel team of nurses. Ours was a supportive and industrious group, working hard every day and often into the evening on our laptops.

My other per diem staffing jobs dwindled during my year-and-a-half with Whole Health Management. I simply did not have time for them. My job in wellness coaching was rewarding — I could see the difference we were making — but it was also time-consuming. My

IBM laptop went home with me almost every night. After fixing dinner, I would often work on projects or try to catch up on email until I went to bed. I was almost never without my laptop, and certainly not when traveling to other sites.

It was during this time with Whole Health Management and Intel that I saw the rapid decline in my mom that I mentioned earlier. Toward the fall of 2007, when I could not even talk with her about returning to her apartment, I knew that the end was near. She had no will to make decisions, no desire to socialize with some of the more alert and friendly residents at her nursing facility. She kept to herself and was miserable.

Because I was traveling so much with my Intel job, I eventually hired one of our clinical assistants to keep Mom company a few days a week in the afternoons. This woman had previously been a nurse's aide and was able to help my mother with some basic needs, but I wanted her mainly just to be with Mom. I think Mom enjoyed this, but she spent most of her days either sleeping or lying in bed staring.

I visited Mom daily when I was home, and I believe my visits brought her comfort. She had always loved music, and I tried to use it to engage her in some activity, but she did not wish to hear any — not even the music she had always loved. I managed to narrow down my trips out of town a bit so I could be with Mom more. I could not be with her all the time, but I was there when my mom turned that last corner and went on to her Lord. I'd like to think she heard me as I sang some familiar hymns to her. That was something I had done for many years, playing the piano and singing, and I think it's a good thing to sing your way home. It was a good thing as well to work with her favorite aide, getting Mom cleaned up one more time and dressing her in an outfit she would have liked for her last trip.

My husband and I decided to move back closer to our kids and grandkids in the fall of 2007 as my mother's health was declining. Knowing my mom would not be with us much longer, we felt in our hearts that we should be handier to the kids. We had settled in New Mexico because that was where we truly wanted to spend the rest of our lives, but our decision was also made with the sense that my mom needed to come live with us in a warmer climate. After she passed away in December of 2007, with another move on both our minds, I began to contemplate ending my job with Whole Health Management when our house sold. In March of 2008, I did leave the wellness program and took a much-needed, month-long break, during which I took care of some of the tasks necessary when a parent dies.

That April I signed with an agency, taking a three-month contract at the VA outpatient clinic in Farmington, New Mexico, up in the Four Corners area. The Navaho Nation occupies a large part of the region, encompassing more than one state, and other Native American tribes are there as well. I had a furnished apartment in Farmington where I lived during the week, and on weekends I made the beautiful three-and-a-half hour drive back to Albuquerque. I loved working with the veterans in this area where New Mexico, Colorado, Utah, and Arizona come together. There were vets from World War II on up. The job was a nice change from Intel's hectic computer-and-meeting-driven wellness program. I went to work at 8:00 a.m. and almost always got out by 5:00 p.m.

The office worked like clockwork. There were enough providers and nurses as well as a lab tech and front office staff. That worked well for the vets. I was truly happy to get back to more of a hands-on nursing job. In many respects, the place was like a mini-hospital; we did all sorts of procedures — whatever we could, as the nearest veterans' hospital was over three hours away in Albuquerque. I worked with some excellent providers and great patients, and thoroughly enjoyed my brief three months there. I enjoyed helping to run the Coumadin Clinic and managing groups of vets with conditions such as hypertension and diabetes. In my spare time, I found the local golf courses and made great women friends from a Thursday evening nine-hole women's league. Playtime is essential!

Our home in Albuquerque sold in July, and by the first few days of August, we were out of New Mexico. I had one more golf tournament to participate in, so Jim and our cat left in our 36-foot motor home, towing his car, and I stayed with a friend a few days longer. We all met up in Michigan, including our daughter and her family, and enjoyed a few days together on the beaches at Saugatuck. Our son was working, so he could not join us in Saugatuck, but after a few days my husband, our cat, and I piled into his home in Portage, where we stayed for a few months.

I applied and interviewed at different healthcare providers in Michigan, but I couldn't get hired for the few months I was willing to stay there, even though I had kept my Michigan license. The employers wouldn't say why, but I believe the reason they were unwilling to hire me short-term had to do with the union contracts most hospitals had by then. Perhaps the unions had clauses that prohibited hiring outsiders at the rate the temporary staffing agencies requested, which could be higher than what the regular hospital employees got paid. Whatever the reason, despite a great track record and superb references from my nursing life, I could not get temporary work even at the hospital in whose OB department I had worked twice. Friends from that hospital were shocked, as they knew the need for fill-in help. But no work. Thus it became even more imperative to find an area to live, move there, and get a job, though not necessarily in that order.

Our son and daughter were each expecting their second child in the fall of 2008, so we were committed to helping out wherever we could as the babies came along. Family first! Finding a new home and area in which to live came second. We had already taken some time to figure out approximately where we would like to live, but we still had some looking to do. We ended up in eastern Tennessee. The terrain, the nearby mountains, and the people we met delighted us, and the lack of a state income tax confirmed our decision. With our son in Michigan and our daughter in northern Virginia, we were determined to locate somewhere within a day's drive of each child. We found just what we were looking for in a superb development south of Knoxville.

Once we had found our home-to-be, I applied and interviewed for hospital staffing work. I figured that would be the quickest way to enter into the area's nursing workforce, and it would also help me determine where I wished to work. I took a job at a local hospital as a float nurse on the night shift for three twelve-hour shifts a week. There were many good nurses there, and I enjoyed the patients; however, I found that the nurse staffing system was not at all what was right for me. It was team leading at its worst. I often had to cover the responsibilities of other caregivers, did not have enough equipment, and could not even begin to leave for home after I had reported to the next shift. My twelve-hour shifts turned into brutally long fourteen-hour shifts.

I had started working at the hospital even before we moved to Tennessee, staying at an extended-stay facility while my husband remained with our son in Michigan until we were ready to move into our home. We did so in mid-November of 2008. It was exciting to once again see all our belongings from New Mexico, which had been in storage since late July. And our move was timed just right! We were able to go to Virginia at the end of the month to help our daughter and family when their second child arrived. My employer graciously worked my schedule to give me the time off I needed. We had welcomed our second grandson into the world the month before; now we were the fond grandparents of four beautiful children!

My job as a float nurse ended sooner rather than later, and not in a way I would have chosen. After leaving work with back spasms that had me limping for about the third time in a row, I started looking for another job. One cropped up quickly, and I took it, eager to move on with work that would help us pay the bills and not be so hard on my back. This job involved handling workers' compensation for a small, local company. It was yet another new adventure which, among its other benefits, was far easier on my back. I found it hard to believe that I only lasted three months at the hospital, but realistically, I should have left sooner before my back gave me fits.

I enjoyed the field of workers' compensation in a way, knowing that we could help smooth the process for the injured and get credible medical reports from the workers' care providers. The workload was sporadic, however, and I was not sure our budget could sustain periods without work. Being a private contractor for the company that hired me was also uncomfortable; I did not like having to save to pay my taxes or the possibility of being terminated at a moment's notice for any reason, at the whim of the employer. So once again I started looking and came across a company I had actually spoken with while we were still in New Mexico, which had operations both there and here in Tennessee.

Professional Case Management cares for the Cold War Patriots: people who experienced daily workplace exposure to toxic chemicals, dust, and other pathogenic substances before much was known about their effects. There are Cold War Patriots all over the country, with heavier concentrations in certain places such as the Oak Ridge, Tennessee, area, where three labs are involved in the nuclear energy industry; and in New Mexico, home to uranium mining and to the Los Alamos National Lab and other nuclear energy labs. Many of the workers in such places have cancers, lung diseases, or neurological diseases that trace directly to exposure to such substances as beryllium, asbestos, and various chemicals.

I have always felt that if you work at something hard enough, things will turn out. Moving from New Mexico temporarily to Michigan and then to East Tennessee, my husband and I fulfilled our twin goals of being available to our two children during the births of their second babies. Nursing is such a great field to be in for so many reasons, but the top one from my standpoint is that I have always been able to do some kind of work-around in order to meet the needs of my family.

My role with Professional Case Managemen allowed me to go back to New Mexico for the summers while staying involved with the company through its spreadsheets, performance improvement tasks, and so on, via my computer. The company was run well from the top down, and its employees did a great job from the bottom up. We were able to keep many Cold War Patriots who qualified for case management and skilled nursing not only in their homes, but in a better and safer, healthier condition than they would have had otherwise. Cold War Veterans can even qualify through the Department of Labor for up to 24/7 skilled nursing care in their homes.

I worked for Professional Case Managemen for about two years while living in East Tennessee. My main job was case management, but I did other jobs as well, including shift work with some of our patients. They were mostly short shifts, but occasionally they included a twelve-hour one. The patients and their families were so grateful for this nursing care, which was provided in their homes by either LPNs or RNs We worked with doctors to confirm to the Department of Labor that the prescribed care hours were truly necessary in order to manage our patients' diseases safely at home, and our patients understood that we had to struggle harder and harder to get those hours approved.

I worked with some amazing caregivers while in Tennessee as well as some memorable patients and their families, some whom remain treasured friends. When we decided to move back to New Mexico permanently in the summer of 2012, I transferred to the Professional Case Management team in Santa Fe as a senior case manager. But the job did not provide the hours I needed with our move back to New Mexico, so I sought other work. And that is how I found perhaps the best company for which I have ever worked — Amerigroup.

In my new capacity, I helped people with financial and physical needs explore their options for personal care services. I also conducted Fair Hearings, held whenever a member appealed the Amerigroup Plan's decision to decrease care hours based on a service coordinator's yearly reassessment. Since the goal of the personal care options is to get people back on their feet to care for themselves whenever possible, I felt that in supporting the Plan's decision, I was representing both the member and the company. The job was interesting and often complex, involving a lot of investigation into the details of each case. The need for long-term coordination of care is badly needed by the growing population of seniors and disabled, many of whom have no other options for the care they need.

At this writing, my passions have run toward working for a brighter future for healthcare and nursing. To me, this means helping to repeal the Patient Protection and Affordable Care Act, more commonly known as ObamaCare, and to establish more workable healthcare initiatives. I did tell you that I was a political science major first, and occasionally that part of me kicks in and I find myself hell-bent on trying to make a difference.

We need to deal with problems such as the current healthcare system and its huge percentage of the GDP. It is a problem not easily solved, but in my opinion it is one that requires more focus on the patients' benefits as opposed to government control of our healthcare. We need to put patients and their physicians and healthcare teams back in control, and I will keep working toward that goal any way that I can.

The very best part is... even though I am currently in the process of retiring, I don't have to look at retirement as permanent. I could change my mind! I can keep my nursing license active, continue to educate myself on current practices, and most importantly, not leave my place of employment with them happy to see the last of me! Even in a profession where there are always needs, it is so important to not burn your bridges. Those bridges should serve to help build a professional track record, not have it crash and burn. If I choose, I can work again on a temporary basis, part-time or full-time, here in New Mexico or elsewhere if I choose. How super is that, to have so many options! I've often thought that the only way I would ever get to visit Australia and see a lot of it is if I took a temporary nursing contract there — and, well, that might be something to think about!

Nurses, I encourage you to always keep informed on the world around you and how it affects your professional well-being. For those who are thinking of becoming a nurse: you have picked a wonderful profession to explore — for it is one that is dedicated to helping others. If I can ever do anything to help you make a decision to go into nursing or another healthcare field, I would be happy to help. Nothing brings a smile to my face faster than having someone tell me they are thinking about nursing school! Helping people is where nursing should be. The cost/benefit analysis is on our side as nurses. We give of ourselves, but we get back so much more.

Thanks for taking my journey with me. And please know that I would love to hear about yours!

Syl

"Make the choice to serve in a cause larger than your wants, larger than yourself— and in your days, you will add not just to the wealth of our country, but to its character."

—George W. Bush, Inauguration Day 2005

About the Author

In *"I Want Chocolate Cake for Dinner!"*, Sylvia Burch shares her passionate, personal adventures in the world of nursing — an exciting vocation filled with opportunities to learn, grow, and make the world a better place.

"Nursing is more than the world's most trusted profession," says Sylvia. "It is also the world's best profession! It is not just for women, it is not the lowest paid profession, and it is not drudgework. It is a pathway to your soul and a roadmap to a bright future."

Forty years in nursing have taken Sylvia across much of America and afforded her a vast array of experiences: part-time and full-time, civilian and military, from staff nurse to administrator and back. The challenges and rewards of a fast-paced labor and delivery unit... the inspiring nobility of wounded warriors at Walter Reed Army Medical Center... the drama and, yes, the humor of neurosurgery — if you've ever wondered what nursing is all about, *"I Want Chocolate Cake for Dinner!"* will give a you a window into one of the most fascinating, diverse, and satisfying vocations anyone can choose.

Sylvia Burch lives in New Mexico with Jim, her treasured husband of almost forty-four years, and their adored cat, Weezy. They have two beautiful children, who have blessed them with four grandchildren — two boys and two girls. Sylvia's passion for taking care of others started early in her life and has never waned. The countless gifts of wisdom and friendship Sylvia has received from her family, friends, coworkers, and patients have guided her life's work. Given any other choice, she would still choose nursing!

Made in the USA
Lexington, KY
22 May 2017